German Military Chaplains
in World War II

German Military
Chaplains
in World War II

Mark Hayden

Schiffer Military History
Atglen, PA

Dedication
This book is dedicated with much love to
Lorraine, Luke, and Daniel
You are my everything—never let go!

Book Design by Ian Robertson.
Copyright © 2005 by Mark Hayden.
Library of Congress Control Number: 2004118317

Printed in China
ISBN: 0-7643-2156-0

We are interested in hearing from authors with book ideas on related topics.

Published by Schiffer Publishing Ltd.
4880 Lower Valley Road
Atglen, PA 19310
Phone: (610) 593-1777
FAX: (610) 593-2002
E-mail: Info@schifferbooks.com.
Visit our web site at: www.schifferbooks.com
Please write for a free catalog.
This book may be purchased from the publisher.
Please include $3.95 postage.
Try your bookstore first.

In Europe, Schiffer books are distributed by:
Bushwood Books
6 Marksbury Avenue
Kew Gardens
Surrey TW9 4JF
England
Phone: 44 (0) 20 8392-8585
FAX: 44 (0) 20 8392-9876
E-mail: Info@bushwoodbooks.co.uk
Free postage in the UK. Europe: air mail at cost.
Try your bookstore first.

Contents

Preface

The subject of military Chaplaincy has always fascinated me. I remember buying a mixed collection of photographs at a militaria fair a number of years ago and one picture caught my eye immediately. It appeared to be a German officer but he had no shoulder straps and was wearing a cross on his chest. Was this really a chaplain and then I asked myself the question that this book attempts to answer – *did Nazi Germany really have military chaplains?*

So began an interest in the area of German military chaplains that has brought me in contact with many collectors over the years. I wish to thank especially Chris Liontas who has kindly opened his vast chaplain collection to me and has been a constant support during this research. Without his input the book would have been a mere shadow of what it is today. A number of other individuals and institutions should also be mentioned with gratitude for their generosity: *Oberst* Adolf Schlicht, Bill Shea, Franco Mesturini, Marineschule Murwik Flensburg, Bundesarchiv, Robert Noss, Mark Bentley, Mick Coverdale, Rick Lundstrom, Bill Dienna, Ian Baxter, Gilles Sigro, Jonathan Maguire, Steve Wolff, Oreste Cassoni, Derek Jones, Justin Horgan, Jurgen Greiner, and Gerard Stezelberger. I also want to thank

Bob Biondi, and Ian Robertson of Schiffer for giving me as much time as I needed to complete the book, and last but not least thank you to my long-suffering family who accepted my disappearing into the office with good grace.

This book is not a textbook, nor is it a definitive work on the subject. It has been written out of a personal desire to find out more about the lives and experiences of German chaplains in World War II. Any mistakes contained herein are the author's fault. I have enjoyed finding so much out about German chaplains – I hope that you the reader will too.

Mark Hayden Spring 2004.

Note
The term Evangelical church, or *Evangelisches Kirche*, refers to the Lutheran members of the Reformed churches. Readers will also encounter the terms Protestant and Episcopalian. All three terms refer to the Lutheran faith, which was the predominant Reformed faith in Germany during the period discussed in this book. Whilst the term *Evangelisches Kirche* does not cover all of the Reformed faiths, it is used for ease of understanding and to spare the reader from being bogged down in theological semantics.

Glossary of Terms

Bolshevism: early name for Communists commonly used in 1920s and 1930s speeches.

Concordat: agreements between the Vatican and another state.

Einheitsfeldmutze: Ski-cap style hat adopted by the German armed forces from 1943 onwards.

Episcopalian: another term for a member of the Reformed churches, usually referring to an Anglican.

Feldgeistlicher: World War I title for an army chaplain: literally translated as field spiritualist- a better term than war priest!

Freikorps: right wing paramilitary groups usually made up of former soldiers who fought against Communist incursion in post World War I Germany. Many went on to become members of the Nazi Party and the SA

Gulag: Russian concentration camp.

Kriegspfarrer: World War II title for an army chaplain: literally translated as war priest, referring usually to chaplains serving for the duration of hostilities.

Messiah: the Holy One who would bring about the Kingdom of God.

Reformation: beginning in the 16th Century, this event heralded the birth of the Protestant churches and changed the world forever.

Reichstag: German seat of government destroyed by fire in 1933.

Soutane: black garment worn by Roman Catholic clergy: similar to the cassock worn by Reformed clergy.

Sturm Abteilung: translates literally as storm detachment but more commonly known as storm troopers. This was the paramilitary arm of the Nazi Party until its emasculation in the Night of the Long Knives in 1934.

Sudeten: refers to a native of the Sudetenland, a region of the northern part of the Czech Republic with a large ethnic German population. Annexed by Germany in October 1938.

Waffen-SS: armed SS. The combat wing of the SS or *Schutz Staffel*: security squad.

1

Introduction

When the subject of German military chaplains comes up in conversation, one can get mixed reactions. The most common reaction is one of incredulity that the country that gave rise to National Socialism would have had priests at all, let alone military chaplains! Such a reaction, however, is to forget that Germany has always been a deeply religious country, and is famous for giving birth to the father of the Reformation Martin Luther. A lot of people find it hard to see beyond the Holocaust and Nazis to the Germany that was still very much in existence during the twelve-year life of the Third Reich.

Many priests and religious (The term priest refers to Diocesan or parish clergy whilst religious refers to priests belonging to a religious order such as the Jesuits.) served as chaplains in the *Wehrmacht* of the Third Reich and many more served as soldiers in medical and front-line regiments. Germany was unusual in that all males of a certain age were eligible to be called up for active service. Being a priest or a member of a religious order or even a seminarian did not prevent a German from being drafted. However, an annex to the Nazi/Vatican Concordat of 1933 governed the treatment of clergy in the event that conscription was enacted in Germany. 'Students studying for the priesthood were declared exempt there from, except in the case of general mobilization. In that event most of the diocesan clergy were to be exempt from reporting for service, while all others were to be inducted for pastoral work with the troops or into the medical corps.'[1] As a result many clergy ended up in uniform as medical personnel and often acted as unofficial chaplains with the tacit approval of their superiors.

A powerful combination of symbols – the German national eagle and Swastika over a Gothic cross of the style worn on a German chaplain's M43 Einheitsfeldmutze. The national cockade is missing but would have been worn under the cross. Courtesy of Chris Liontas.

Reichswehr troops on church parade in the early 1930s. Church parades were a normal part of the soldier's routine. Author.

A photograph that indicates how the Nazis would have liked things to be in a post Christian Reich: a commanding officer performs a marriage service for one of his soldiers whilst the bride, back in Germany, also attends a civil ceremony! Courtesy of Bill Shea.

A valid question has arisen time and again during the research for this book: how could a priest serve as a chaplain when the Nazis were persecuting the church that he served. This is a question that will need to be looked at in depth during the course of this book. It is on record that despite assurances from them in the early 1930s, the Nazis intended to replace Christianity with their own creed and form of worship. How then could so many priests don the field gray or navy blue and serve a regime that ultimately wished to see the priesthood and religion removed?

As previously stated, chaplains served in almost every theatre of operations of the German armed forces yet some people still doubt their existence. During the research for this book I have turned up many interesting and unusual photographs of chaplains on active service. I have also found evidence of a uniformed *Luftwaffe* chaplain, even though the *Luftwaffe* did not officially have chaplains. There is also anecdotal evidence of a *Waffen-SS* chaplain but more about this later. I have also collated a number of photographs of the chaplains serving with some of Germany's Axis allies.

Above and Following: A trio of photographs taken during the visit of the Cardinal Archbishop of Munich, Dr. Franziskus von Bettinger to Bavarian troops at Brainville in France in 1916. A visit like this could be a morale booster and also took place during World War II, in spite of Party efforts to undermine the position of the hierarchy. Courtesy of Rick Lundstrom.

The aim of this book is to try and learn more about the world of the German chaplain of World War II. How did he serve a regime as corrupt as the Third Reich? What was the relationship like between the churches and the Nazis? What was the training to be a chaplain like? How was he distinguished as a chaplain? What were his duties? How did the chaplain cope with the war, defeat and the realization of the true nature of the Nazi Final Solution? I hope to look at these issues and more in the course of this book.

This book has arisen out of a desire to learn more about the actions of the clergy in Germany during the Third Reich and especially the role of the military chaplain. I will raise uncomfortable questions in this book and this is done out of a sense of love for the churches in which I have served both as a Roman Catholic and Episcopalian priest. I would ask you the reader to set aside any preconceptions you might have until you have finished reading this book and then I would ask you to answer this question; how might you have acted as a Christian living in Germany between 1933 and 1945?

2

Church and State Relations

As with any historical work, the author and reader view the subject from out of their respective experiences and naturally from a position of distance from the events being discussed. When looking at Church-State relations in the Third Reich we must suspend our own opinions in order to be able to place ourselves in the mind of the average German Christian who lived through the years of the Third Reich. Only by doing this can we attempt to understand the moral dilemma faced by the 'person in the pew.'

One needs to appreciate the mood in Germany after World War I. A poem of the time, long before Hitler appeared, captures the need for a leader; 'O God, send us a *Führer* who will change our misfortune by God's word.'[2] This shows how ripe Germany was for a leader to appear and take control in a Germany that was still in shock from defeat, economic depression and revolution. Nationalism and religion were comfortable bedfellows for many Germans of the day and if a leader came and promised the German people regained self-respect, prosperity and religious freedom, then that leader was sure to gain a very favourable hearing from the masses.

Adolf Hitler was a dynamic speaker, few can doubt that. He evoked strong feelings in many people, either positive or negative. However, it is amazing to read the accounts of the time in which people confer an almost God-like quality to the Führer. Indeed many turned their backs on God and replaced Him with the new Messiah-Hitler. Adolf Hitler always believed that he had a divine mission to Germanize the world and create a 'New World Order' with himself as the figurehead. The churches faced difficulties with the Nazis from the outset in that many of the faithful were turning their backs on the 'Jewish' Christ and embracing the new Aryan Creed. The Bible was used in anti Jewish classes and the false

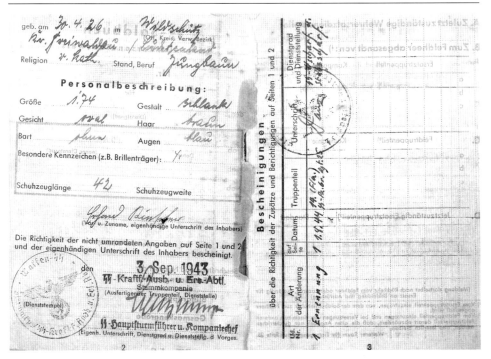

Page 2 of a Waffen-SS Soldbuch that identifies the soldier as a Roman Catholic. All members of the SS were required to believe in God – just one of the many paradoxes to be found during the course of a study of religion in Nazi Germany. Courtesy of Justin Horgan.

tale of Gentiles being used in blood sacrifice by Jews in Europe in the past was resurrected again. Jews were also referred to as the killers of Christ in an attempt to rouse up anti Jewish feeling amongst devout Christians.

Some of those who held onto their faith wondered if God had sent Hitler to deliver them from the hardships of recession and to stem the tide of Bolshevism. A Sudeten German asked 'Maybe Jesus sent that man Hitler into our land to bring an end to the depression. Things couldn't get any worse than they are now.'[3] A strange question in light of the war and the Holocaust but this question was asked in 1938 when many Sudeten Germans found life hard in Czechoslovakia and were treated like long lost family when the Germans annexed the Sudetenland in October 1938.

Shortly after becoming Chancellor in 1933, Adolf Hitler made a speech in the Reichstag during which he made the following statement; 'The national government sees in the two Christian confessions most vital factors in the survival of our nationality. Their rights shall not be touched. The national government will accord and secure to the Christian confessions the influence that is due them in schools and education. The battle against a nationalistic world concept and the struggle for a real national unity serves the interests of the nation

A religious memorial card (traditional in the Roman Catholic faith) to an Army chaplain – Johann Liedl – who was killed whilst serving as a Divisional Chaplain in Russia in August 1942. Courtesy of Chris Liontas.

just as much as those of our Christian faith.'[4] This speech took place in the Reichstag on March 23, 1933. It is easy to see how leading church figures committed themselves in support of the new regime after such a pro-church statement. The church leaders held the hope (false as it turned out) that National Socialism would defend the rights of Christianity and act as a bulwark against the encroaching evil of Bolshevism.

However, in spite of this promise, it was not long before the apparatus of the Third Reich began to work its way into German society at every level and undermine the authority and position of the churches. The erosion of the Protestant and Roman Catholic Churches was one of the ultimate goals of the Nazi party. The minister appointed by the *Führer* as Minister for Church Affairs – Hans Kerrl – made a statement shortly after his appointment that held an ominous premonition for the future of Church-State relations.

'There is a new authority arisen in Germany which will say what Christ and Christianity means for Germans. That authority is Adolf Hitler.[5]

Thus began a huge interference in church affairs by the state far in excess of that by the ultramontane Chancellor Bismarck in the 19th Century. Church youth groups were closed down; clergy were imprisoned, censured and assaulted. False charges were made against leading Christians. Church property was seized and religious education in schools had to follow the new state curriculum with its emphasis on race, nation and German supremacy. The opinion of the National Socialists was that the churches were to place themselves, without reserve, at the service of the state and become subject to its new political and spiritual leader.[6] The fact that many Christian leaders and faithful did so is a matter of record.

The Christian group that was most pro-establishment was the group known as the German Christians. They were drawn from the *Evangelische Kirche* (Lutheran Church), and were organized under the counsel and advice of the Führer. This group, quite unlike any other Christian group 'were supported by the National Socialist party, by the State, its officials and the police.[7] Ludwig Mueller was elected as Bishop and head of the German Christian movement. Bishop Mueller was a former *Kaiserliche Marine* Chaplain and was highly decorated in World War I, receiving both the Iron Cross 1st Class and the Friedrich August Cross 1st Class. Shortly after his election as Bishop, the Prussian General Synod, which was dominated by the German Christians, ratified a proposal that any future holder of a clerical office should be of Aryan ancestry.[8] This ratification led to virulent protests from the majority of the Evangelical churches and eventually led to the founding of the Confessional Church. This group took a firm stance against the German Christians and their barely disguised masters. At one point in the mid 1930s nearly 10,000 of the 18,000 Evangelical priests had enrolled in the Confessional Church. This brave witness was not without cost as many of the priests of the Confessional Church languished in prison and concentration camps for the duration of Nazi rule and many paid the ultimate price for their witness against Nazism.

The leading spokesman for the Confessional Church was also a naval veteran of World War I- Martin Niemoller who had been a distinguished U-boat commander during the war and entered religious life afterwards. He had initially supported the new regime but like others once he realized what the true Nazi agenda was he became an outspoken critic of the Nazis. Niemoller served as Pastor in Dahlem, a village outside Berlin. From 1937 onwards, Pastor Niemoller was 'arrested, imprisoned, set free, rearrested, and sent to concentration camps'.[9] He joined many of his fellow priests in the concentration camps and Pastor Niemoller was the one who declared that the German Christians were heretical and contrary to the teachings of Christ. He is best known for an often repeated quotation; 'When they came for the Jews I said nothing because I wasn't a Jew, when they came for the gypsies, I said nothing because I wasn't a gypsy, when they came for the Catholics I said nothing because I wasn't a Catholic. When they came for me, nobody said anything because nobody was left.' Martin Niemoller was fortunate to be liberated by Allied troops from Dachau Concentration camp in 1945. His fellow pastor and critic of the Third Reich, Dietrich Bonhoeffer was executed at Flossenburg in the last days of the war.

Above and following: In stark contrast to the religious memorial card is this notice recording the death of an Army Pionier – who is pictured with his family. This notice contains no reference whatsoever to God but states that, true to his oath as a German soldier, he laid down his life for Fuhrer, Volk and Fatherland. Author.

Am 2. 8. 43 erhielten wir die unfaßbare, tieftraurige Nachricht, daß mein über alles geliebter, treusorgender Mann, meiner beiden Kinder herzensguter Papi, unser lieber, hoffnungsvoller einziger Sohn, Schwiegersohn, Bruder, Schwager und Onkel, der Reichsangestellte

Pionier

Hermann Senne

am 20. 7. 43 bei den schweren Abwehrkämpfen nordwestlich Orel schwer verwundet und einige Stunden später auf einem Hauptver-bandplatz seinen Verletzungen kurz vor seinem 37. Geburtstag er-legen ist. Getreu seinem Fahneneid gab auch er sein Leben für Führer, Volk und Reich. Am 21. 7. 43 wurde er unter militärischen Ehren auf einem Heldenfriedhof beigesetzt

In unsagbarem Schmerz

Elfriede Senne
geb. Lampe

Manfred und Hannelore
als Kinder

Hermann Lambeck und Frau Amanda
verw. Senne

Wwe. Elfriede Lampe
geb Bunke

Walter Denecke und Frau Amanda
geb. Senne

Uffz. Bernhard Lampe und Frau Margarethe
zzt. im Osten   geb. Kielhorn

5 kleine Neffen und Nichten

Gifhorn, Hitzacker/Elbe, Gut Langenberg,
über Stettin
Fallingbostel, den 6. August 1943

After their rejection of the Nazi worldview, the Confessional Church underwent severe repression. Indeed the members of the Confessional Church only knew each other by face, not by name, in an attempt to limit the risk from the authorities. This repression eventually led to the Confessional Church going underground and it seemed as if official resistance to the regime had ceased. There is an aspect to all of this that is hard to understand in light of what we know today. Many of the priests languishing in prison remained loyal to the state and were quite prepared to do their duty if required of them. Many held the belief that the *Führer* was unaware of the conduct of some of his functionaries and if the clergy remained faithful, surely better times would follow.

In November 1937, the Evangelical Army chaplains wrote a letter to the *Führer* protesting at the treatment of the church and its members. This is part of the text; 'Protestant Christians, in spite of all that they have experienced, will do their duty in time of war. Of that there can be no doubt.'[10] The letter was ignored by the *Führer* yet when war came, many pastors volunteered as military chaplains in spite of the fact that many of the pastors in prison were themselves highly decorated World War I chaplains.[11] Their crime? Not complying with the will of the *Führer* and the party to impose their warped ideals on the people.

The Pastor of Hell-Fire! In this picture we see GFM Rommel with Major Wilhelm Bach, a commander of the 104th Artillery Regiment who distinguished himself at Halfaya Pass. He was in peacetime an Evangelische Pastor from Mannheim! Not all clergy served as chaplains or medical personnel! Courtesy of Oreste Cassoni.

The State gradually began to extend its influence in areas that had been traditionally the preserve of the churches – a civil marriage takes place under the watchful gaze of the Fuhrer. Author.

In all, the German Christian movement gained little support amongst the people and were viewed by the majority of Christians as Nazi lackeys. Indeed Mueller was nicknamed the 'Brown Bishop', presumably comparing him to the brown shirted storm troopers. On the other hand the sacrifice of the Confessional Church both at home and at the front was huge. Post-war the Protestant churches struggled with the ghosts of its Nazi past and failure to organize effective resistance to Nazi oppression. A sad fact is that those who are quick to condemn the churches for moral impotence during the Third Reich have largely forgotten the bravery of the Confessional Church against the Nazis.

The Roman Catholic Church in Germany faced a somewhat different situation than that faced by the Reformed Churches. The persecution of the Roman Catholic Church was very severe because of its international nature and the fact that the Roman Catholic faithful gave their loyalty to a foreign head of state – the Pope. This view is borne out by the experiences of an American airman who was shot down over Germany in November 1944. Lieutenant Radnossky sustained injuries from anti-aircraft fire and also whilst bailing out of his crippled B-17. He was captured and taken to a Roman Catholic civilian hospital in Dechta. He was well looked after by all the staff who ignored the fact that he was Jewish, a fact easily discovered by reading his dog tags. Lt. Radnossky made friends with many of the staff and his opinion was, 'thinking back, the most important thing was that these people were Catholic first and then Germans.'[12] This is exactly what the National Socialists feared and why they moved to weaken the hold the Roman Catholic Church had over the faithful. However strong the faith of the people was, many Roman Catholics were willing supporters of the National Socialists and some of the most senior party members were or had been Roman Catholics themselves. The birthplace of National Socialism, Bavaria, is located in the predominantly Catholic south of Germany.

Those members of the Roman Catholic faith who resisted the Nazis from the beginning were left with little or no grounds for argument after Nazi Germany signed a Concordat with the Vatican in 1933. This signing was the result of many years of work both on Germany's and the Vatican's behalf. Initialed on July 9th and signed on July 20th, the Concordat was ratified and came into law on September 10, 1933 The German military had for a long time wanted to appoint an army bishop with responsibility for all military chaplains. The situation as it stood saw the chaplains obliged to seek permission, or dispensation, to conduct various sacramental duties from the local priest or bishop. If the Vatican ratified the appointment of a military bishop, he could grant the faculties (powers) required to allow the military chaplains full autonomy in their duties. The Vatican sought guarantees from the new government with regard to state payments to the church, protection of the rights of church school's, cease the persecution of clergy and guarantee church property.

In order for the National Socialists to agree to the Concordat, which allowed Canon Law (the internal law of the Roman Catholic Church) to be imposed fully on German Roman Catholics, Hitler, as well as pushing for the military bishop demanded 'the voluntary withdrawal of German Catholics from social and political action *as Catholics'*.[13] This robbed the average German Roman Catholic of an effective basis for protest because to continue to protest as a Catholic, one was disobeying the ruling of the Roman Catholic Church! Roman Catholics were now permitted to be members of the Nazi party without fear of censure from the church. Sadly, the man who acted on behalf of the Vatican, Cardinal Pacelli, did so without open consultation of the German faithful. He negotiated with the then Vice Chancellor Franz von Papen, himself a Roman Catholic and former leader of the Catholic Centre Party. This role did not mitigate against Pacelli in later life as he went on to become Pope Pius the Twelfth and his secretary went on to become Pope Paul the Sixth. Much has been written about the pre-war and wartime actions or inactions of Pope Pius XII but suffice it to say that he saw the true threat to Europe and his church as coming from the influence of Soviet Russia. He truly believed that European nationalism was the bulwark that would save Christendom from a new dark age. To comment further about Pope Pius the XII's wartime conduct is beyond the subject of this work.

Article 27 of the Concordat is relevant to our study. In it 'the government achieved its wish for an exempt pastoral ministry for the German army, headed by an army bishop to be selected by mutual agreement of the Reich government and the Holy See. The German episcopate was given some control over the military clergy by the provision that only priests who had the approval of their local bishop for such pastoral work could be appointed as

The outside of a registry office adorned with Nazi signs – a Luftwaffe man and his bride after their marriage ceremony. Author.

A Waffen-SS officer and his wife leaving a church after being married – one would presume incorrectly – that the SS would have embraced the Nazi civil service far more readily, but this appears not to be the case. Courtesy of Justin Horgan.

military chaplains. (This stipulation is the norm for all clergy applying to be military chaplains today.) An Apostolic Brief, to be formulated in co-operation with the Reich, was to regulate these matters in detail.'[14] To delve further into this period is again beyond the scope of this work but it is important to note that the Holy See willingly allowed the various Catholic parties to be emasculated by the National Socialists in return for guarantees that turned out to be empty promises. The historian of the Centre party, Karl Bachem, no doubt expressed the views of many when he wrote in his diary, "After the bishops unanimously have professed their recognition of the new government, such resistance for us would have been morally unjustifiable and impossible. We have no choice but to follow the example of the bishops.'[15] Perhaps this begins to cast light on the recurring question of postwar writers as to why the churches did so little in the face of the evil that was National Socialism.

The charge of complete collusion with the Nazi regime has been leveled at the Christian churches in Germany and especially at the Roman Catholic Church after the events described above. To accept this charge as fact is a dangerous and naïve undertaking. We must recognize that the position taken by the German churches to the Third Reich was one of 'mixed support and opposition.'[16] Such a statement requires the reader to stop for a moment and take a look at the Germany and on a wider scale the Europe that spawned nationalism in its various forms from the 1920s onwards. Europe after World War I was a much-changed place in terms of political structures. Many of the royal houses that had ruled pre war Europe had fallen victim to the upheaval of the war and a new political system was beginning to emerge in Russia. Bolshevism was beginning to take hold after the 1917 revolution. Despite valiant efforts by the White Russians, aided by some Western countries, the Russian Civil War ended with the Bolsheviks triumphant.

As unemployment and disillusionment took hold in post war Europe, the socialist promises of all men as equals and the setting up of a workers paradise held great attractions for many of the returning soldiers and the people who had been affected most by the war. Bolshevism also found a warm welcome in many parts of Germany and *Freikorps* units were raised in an attempt to prevent a complete Bolshevik take over in the Reich. (The *Freikorps* were right wing groups, mostly made up of former soldiers, who took up arms and organized resistance to the increasing Bolshevik movement in Germany and also protected the country from border incursions in the East, mainly on the frontier with Poland.) The key point for this study is that Bolshevism, at its most basic level, relegates religion to nothing more than a means by which capitalists and monarchs control the masses. As the German philosopher Karl Marx once wrote, 'religion is the opium of the people.' The Bolsheviks called for dissolution of the churches and an end to religious practice. This soon became the norm in the new Soviet Russia and many church leaders looked on in horror as churches were turned into storehouses and priests and people sent to gulags (Soviet concentration camps) for continuing to practice their faith.

Chriſtliches Andenken
im Gebete

an den

Alumnus des 4. theologiſchen Kurſes

Herrn Pius Leitner

Obergefreiter der Luftwaffe

Inhaber des E. K. II

geboren am 29. April 1916
gefallen am 15. Februar 1942
in Rußland.

R. I. P.

Wir empfehlen Dir, o Gott, die Seele Deines
Dieners, welcher im chriſtlichen Glauben und in der
Hoffnung auf Deine große Barmherzigkeit aus dieſem
Leben geſchieden iſt. Nimm ihn gnädig zu Dir auf,
damit er ſelig bei Dir auch für uns fürbitte, die wir
hienieden ſeiner in Liebe gedenken. Durch Jeſum
Chriſtum unſern Herrn. Amen.

Mein Jeſus Barmherzigkeit!

(300 Tage Ablaß.)

Buchdruckerei Max Herzog, Rottenburg

Zum treuen Gedenken im Gebete
an meinen lieben, braven Sohn,
unser unvergeßliches Bruderherz

Alfons Aßfalg

Sanitäts-Unteroffizier

geboren am 16. Mai 1918
in Altheim/Riedlingen
gefallen am 25. Januar 1945
bei Klein Gnie (Ostpreußen)

Meine Brüder! Wir wollen euch nicht
in Ungewißheit lassen über die Entschlafenen, damit ihr nicht trauert
wie die andern, die keine Hoffnung
haben. Wenn Jesus, wie wir glauben,
gestorben und auferstanden ist, so
wird Gott auch die Entschlafenen
durch Jesus herbeiführen mit ihm.

(1. Thess. 4, 12—13.)

Den Christusgläubigen wird das Leben
nicht genommen, vielmehr neu geschenkt
Zerfällt die Herberge dieses Erdenlebens
in Staub, so öffnet sich das Vaterhaus im
Himmel auf ewig

GEBETSANDENKEN
an den Herrn

Johann Fürst in Unterhüttensölden

Gefreiter in einem Gebirgsjäger - Regiment
Priesteramtskandidat des philosophischen Kurses
Alumnus des Bischöflichen Klerikalseminars
St. Stephan in Passau

Er gab sein junges, hoffnungsvolles Leben am 1. Oktober 1941 im Kampfe fürs Vaterland in der Ukraine

BUCHDRUCKEREI OTTO MORSAK, GRAFENAU

Dem Gedenken

im hl. Meßopfer und dem Gebete der
Gläubigen wird empfohlen die Seele

des

Hochwürdigen Herrn

Franz Krautgartner

Er durfte am 29. Juni 1938 die heil.
Priesterweihe empfangen und am
4. Juli sein erstes heil. Meßopfer in
seiner Heimat Alkoven darbringen.
Nachdem er als Kooperator in Gries-
kirchen, Steyr und Königswiesen
eifrigst gewirkt, wurde er am 6. De-
zember 1940 zum Sanitätsdienst ein-
berufen. Am 16. Oktober 1944 nach
schweren Kämpfen in Belgrad ge-
fangen, wurde der 31jährige Priester
am selben Tag mit vielen Kameraden,
denen er noch unmittelbar vor dem
bitteren Todesgang die General-
absolution und seinen priesterlichen
Segen erteilt hatte, ein Opfer der
Partisanen.

It was a simple movement of opinion that allowed the Christian churches to fall in with the right wing nationalism that was growing in Europe. The nationalists were virulently anti Bolshevik and many were devout members of their churches as well. An unsavoury fact for the Christian churches today is the fact that many clergy preached strong sermons against Bolshevik Russia and the dangers of the 'red tide' threatening to engulf Europe. For example, when the Spanish Civil War broke out many Europeans flocked to join the Republican side to fight against Fascism but a large number also went to fight on the Nationalist side against Bolshevism. Some went as committed Fascists but others went to defend Mother Church in Spain from the 'evil Reds' backed by Moscow. Many priests in my own country preached that it was the Christian duty of young men to go and fight in Spain against the 'Godless Communists' and those who fought for the Republicans were often excommunicated for their 'act of betrayal' to the faith. An elderly colleague told me of sitting in Mass

Above: A picture sure to stir up some comment! Here is a chaplain taking a funeral service but dressed in the uniform of a Luftwaffe Non Commissioned Officer. It is on record that the Luftwaffe had no appointed chaplains as it was an organization strongly controlled by the Nazi Party. This priest was obviously drafted into the Luftwaffe but has been allowed to act as a chaplain, along with his other duties by his commanding officer. Regardless of Party influence, fallen Luftwaffe men needed funerals too! Note the non-regulation cross-worn on the front of the tunic. Courtesy of William Dienna. Opposite: Four examples of memorial cards to priests who fell whilst serving but not as chaplains – two served as medics, one as a mountain trooper, and one served in the Luftwaffe. Many clergy died in action after being drafted into the armed forces.

in the late 1930s and the priest leading the people in prayer for Adolf Hitler who was holding back the tide of Communism from the Christian world!

When Generalissimo Franco's forces finally prevailed in Spain, many churches rang their bells throughout Europe and many Masses were said in thanksgiving for what was seen as God's victory over the Godless. One question though: what about all the poor souls killed in places like Guernica and Barcelona? Who said Mass for all the innocent victims of the war?

Many of the charges leveled at the Communists by the churches were in turn to come true in Nazi Germany. There was no place in Hitler's worldview for religion and priests yet he courted the clergy until such time he had gained absolute power. Even when the Nazis were hard pressing the churches, the hierarchy only ever spoke out when issues such as education or euthanasia were being raised. The churches objected to the interference by the state in their schools and also objected to the T4 programme, which was 'cleansing' German society of genetic defects by killing those deemed to be genetically inferior. However, why didn't the churches speak out at the now commonplace deportations of Jews and other non-desirables to the concentration camps? Foreign church leaders knew about the camps and did nothing even though they were safe from the Gestapo (*Geheime Staats Polizei*) The

A funeral on the Western Front in August 1944. It is being conducted by the soldier second from the left. He is likely to be a priest/soldier drafted into a medical unit who acted as an unofficial chaplain with the tacit approval of his CO. he wears the uniform of an Obergefreiter and is only identifiable as a priest by his stole and prayer book. Author.

hardest fact that a Christian has to accept is that the churches were weak in the face of adversity, in spite of the brave witness by many individuals.

This section ends with a look at one of the recurring questions from the Third Reich-how could Christians serve as instruments of the Nazis and do unspeakable acts and not rebel against their leaders? A partial answer lies in the oath taken by every German service-man during the Third Reich. The oath to serve ones country was as sacred to the German military as professing one's faith in church and Hitler was well aware of this when he introduced the new oath for the *Wehrmacht* in 1934. The text of this new oath, which was printed in the German soldier's prayer book, is as follows;

'*I swear before God this sacred oath that I will render unconditional obedience to the Führer of the German nation and Volk, Adolf Hitler, the supreme commander of the armed forces and that, as a brave soldier, I will be ready at all times to stake my life in fulfillment of this oath.*'

No matter what the beliefs of the fallen, all deserved a place to rest. This picture shows the last gesture to a fallen comrade on the eastern Front. The graves of Axis troops rarely survived the wrath of the advancing Red Army. Author.

The Iron Cross used as a grave marker whilst the Christian Cross stands in the centre of a military graveyard – an excellent example of secular and sacred sharing the same space. Author.

The churches accepted the Nazis as the legitimate authority in Germany and exhorted their faithful to remain true to the State, even as evidence of state sanctioned religious persecution grew. The oath was used to tie the German soldier in holy obedience to the *Führer* and a number of clergy referred to this oath in postwar interviews as an explanation for their service as chaplains during the war. Many officers found themselves unable to act against Hitler because of this oath. Indeed many of the conspirators who planned the July 20, 1944 bomb attack on Hitler were condemned as traitors for breaking their oath as officers, even though they were acting for the good of Germany! Archbishop Conrad Grober of Freiburg even went so far as to round on the Allies who condemned German Roman Catholics for apparent moral cowardice during the Third Reich when in October 1945 he questioned if mutiny could be reconciled with the sacred oath taken by all in the military: 'One should not forget the horrible fate of all, including the highest ranking generals, who dared to speak of peace and an end to the war or who tried to eliminate the driving force behind the war by means of assassination. In this connection, we German Catholics know the judgement of our church regarding tyrannicide which she forbids just as she forbids murder in general.'[17] The senior Roman Catholic army chaplain, Bishop Josef Rarkowski summed up the essence of the oath as follows: 'The soldierly calling is distinguished from all other professions and tasks in this: that once the oath of allegiance has been sworn, it demands the heroic dedication of body and soul and elevates this dedication to a conscious and inflexible principle. Thus the military training program to which you have been called at the will of the Supreme Commander represents the highest service to *Volk and Vaterland*.'[18]

How hard it must have been for any effective resistance to the regime for the average Christian when the church leaders at the highest levels were seen to be pro-Hitler, to greater and lesser extents. Indeed it was also impossible for a person to avoid military service by claiming to be a conscientious objector. Conscientious objection was viewed in the First World War as cowardice and indeed many were imprisoned because of their stance. However, with the passage of time, conscientious objectors were recognized as deeply committed people. Many served bravely on the Allied side as medics and stretcher-bearers. However, the case was far different in Nazi Germany. Conscientious objection was unfairly classed as treason against the State and the sentence was death by beheading. The true reasons why a man refused to serve would never be revealed and the party would be sure to fabricate some terrible charge which would destroy the reputation of the mans family. The widow of Franz Jaegerstatter, an Austrian peasant executed for conscientious objection to military service, stated that many of the people living in the rural village from which he came still resented the fact that her husband had not been a soldier.[19] The average German Roman Catholic who decided to refuse military service would have received no support whatsoever from his spiritual leaders.[20] Indeed, *Herr* Jaegerstatter was challenged by his Bishop over his refusal to serve and said that an individual had no right to 'reach such a judgement nor take such a stand.' This attitude is frightening to us today and yet the people in *Herr* Jaegerstatter's village still persisted in their attitudes towards this brave man *20 years after the war was over!*

Interestingly, there are now moves afoot to beatify *Herr* Jaegerstatter, the first step to sainthood. One of this brave man's final statements is brutal in its honesty and must be reflected upon by all Christians today; 'If the church stays silent in the face of evil, what difference would it make if no church were ever opened again?' One can presume that this statement will not be read out at the beatification ceremony in Rome!

A Waffen-SS graveyard – identified by the use of the Nordic death rune as a grave marker. However, the Iron Cross and Christian Cross again take centre place in the graveyard. Author.

3

The Role of the Chaplain

The role of a military chaplain is the same no matter what branch of service he/she serves in. The only differences are usually either cultural or denominational. Whilst wearing the uniform of the service in which he is serving, the chaplain is first and foremost a man of God and it is important that he is easily recognizable as a chaplain. The uniforms and accoutrements of the chaplain will be discussed later. This section of the book is to give the reader a brief overview of the duties of a chaplain in order to give a better understanding of the photographs in the book.

The primary role of the chaplain is to provide for the spiritual needs of the soldiers both in the field and behind the lines. This would usually mean conducting the religious services common to each denomination. For Roman Catholic chaplains this normally meant celebrating Mass daily (where circumstances permitted) and distributing Communion to the sick and wounded in hospital. Another large part of the Roman Catholic chaplains role was to hear the confessions of the soldiers prior to going into action or very often whilst at the front! Episcopal chaplains generally celebrated Holy Communion once a week but also held services of Morning and Evening Prayer on a regular basis with various groups of soldiers. The chaplains would also be available to pray with the men should the need arise. The chaplains would also conduct other sacramental duties such as baptisms and weddings but usually these happy events took place back at the home garrison or well in the rear of the lines. However sometimes the sacraments took place in the most unusual surroundings: 'Once Padre Peter's celebrated a baptism. In one of the huts (at Gumrak Field Hospital outside Stalingrad) there lay a soldier, the son of working people from Altona, a lad of twenty-three with an injury to his spine, who begged to be christened. He also begged the

Above: A chaplain in conversation with two officers. One of the most important roles of the chaplain is to act as a link between the officers and men. Courtesy of Chris Liontas.

Left: A chaplain performing a marriage ceremony between a uniformed couple. Note that the chaplain wears his uniform instead of ecclesiastical robes whilst performing the marriage. Bundesarchiv.

A chaplain baptizing an infant outdoors – unusual in itself, as baptisms usually take place in church. Again, the ceremony is conducted by the chaplain in military uniform. Note that a soldier is holding the child and the chaplain is assisted by another soldier. Bundesarchiv.

Chaplains were usually attached to a military hospital, either behind the lines or a field hospital near the front line. This early photograph shows two part-time chaplains in clerical dress in conversation with a doctor and a SanitatsFeldwebel (medical NCO) Author.

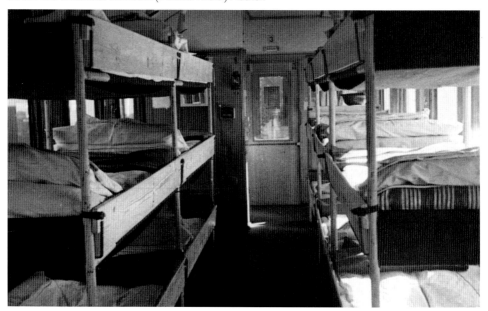

As the front lines grew the need for hospital trains became apparent, and a carriage like this one was often the workplace for a chaplain. This train was photographed enroute from Warsaw to Linz in July 1943. Author.

Padre not to tell his father in Germany who would be annoyed. Peter's lit a candle and baptized him with due ceremony, and the others in the room who looked on were touched, or embarrassed or just curious.'[21]

It could be an uphill struggle for some of the chaplains because many of the soldiers they ministered to had grown to maturity on a diet of National Socialist thought and opinion and many had turned their backs on organized religion completely. One incident bears this point out and is stark in its portrayal of the growing desperation felt by the German soldier on the Eastern Front: 'My best friend was caught there (Stalingrad) Kurt had a far-away stare. We do not know yet if he died or was captured. But we have whispered tales among us that when the Russians closed the ring and we couldn't get through with food or mail any-more except by air, that one of the last wireless messages we got from within was the call '*Send us Bibles! Send us Bibles!*' Hansi, why on earth did our boys call for Bibles to help them die? I don't know much what a Bible is like; isn't it a Jewish book of some sort? Did they give them Bibles? Yes, they dropped all the Bibles that could be found. There were not many around you know. One fellow who escaped after capture told me that our soldiers would beg for just one page to hold in their hands.'[22] In this world where some soldiers didn't even know what a Bible was ministered the army chaplain.

The chaplain was a welcome change from the doctors, but a more welcome sight were the nurses who tended to the wounded. Author.

A chaplain celebrating Mass for the troops at an altar bedecked with Swastika flags and under the gaze of a Fuhrer portrait. Many chaplains were uncomfortable after the war to admit to having used the Kriegsfahne (War flag) in services. Courtesy of HITM.

A field altar being prepared for Mass in a quiet area of the front. Note the altar drape with the Imperial Iron Cross on the front of it – a traditional symbol with strong links to the Prussian past. Courtesy of Chris Liontas.

Chaplains also provided services for the local population if their priest was not present. This happened quite a lot in White Russia and the Ukraine where religious practice had been suppressed under the Soviet regime. Many of the Orthodox churches had been used as storehouses and barns under the Soviets but with the advance of the Axis forces, many villages began to practice their religion again. This led to the initial welcoming of the Germans and their Allies as liberators. This feeling did not last long after the *Einsatzgruppen* and *Sonderkommando* of the SS arrived after the front line troops had moved on. It then became a case of swapping one sadistic godless master for another.

Sadly, a large portion of the chaplain's time would be taken up with the preparation for and conducting of funeral services for the fallen. Some of the photographs found in this book show elaborate funerals with all the trappings that armies attach to the funerals of their fallen. However, in frontline areas, all that a chaplain could do was to give a dying man the last rites and retrieve a portion of his dog tag in order to record the soldier's death. Once the fighting was over, the dead would be recovered and a proper funeral would take place but as the tide of war turned against Germany, very often all a soldier could hope for was that his death would be recorded and the information passed on to his loved ones. (Even the resting places of fallen Axis soldiers did not survive the vengeful Red Army in its advance on Germany.) A good example of this practice of recording the details of the fallen is a story told in Berlin during the fierce fighting in 1945 and can be found in James Lucas's book 'Last Days of the Reich;' 'We had a military chaplain with us in the (flak) tower who was worried because he could not record the details of the fallen. If he could not report these correctly and report them to the proper authority the dead would be merely listed as missing.'[23] Many people will know the pain of being told that a loved one is missing in action and the chaplains provided a vital service in recording the names of the dead so that their families would know the fate of their beloved son or husband. Garrison chaplains also had the grim task of breaking the news to families of the death of a loved one.

German chaplains were usually attached to medical units of field hospitals and were also on the staff of the larger hospitals. The chaplain's role here was to provide pastoral care to the wounded. Visitors were very scarce in a field hospital for obvious reasons and so the chaplain was the only visitor many of the soldiers had. Regardless of how religious or irreligious they were, many of the soldiers were glad to get a break from the medical staff and have someone to talk to and perhaps write a letter home for them so that they could let the family know they were recovering. *Herr* Monsignor Alois Beck who served with the 6th Army in Stalingrad spent a lot of his time performing these tasks for the wounded until contact with the outside world was lost. The chaplain also helped the medical staff as best he could; 'Instead of saying Mass, I held heads and gave shots.'[24] The chaplain could also pull strings and get a wounded man a place on a plane or train home as most chaplains built up a good rapport with the doctors at a field hospital. Life was hard for the frontline chap-

An Evangelisches chaplain preaching a sermon in the Low Countries in 1940. The Iron Cross on the altar drape is of the style of the decoration itself. The Iron Cross was clearly a popular and accepted image in the eyes of the clergy. Courtesy of Chris Liontas.

lain as he was dealing primarily with the wounded and dying. Many chaplains found it hard to keep going but did so nonetheless; 'I was the Catholic priest of the 96th Infantry Division in Stalingrad. On November 22, 1942, the encirclement was completed. It was a month during which I closed the eyes of about 1,000 young German soldiers.'[25] Accounts like these put the role of the frontline chaplain into perspective.

An unpleasant task, which could often fall to the chaplain, was to accompany condemned men to their place of execution. The chaplain was very often the only visitor that a prisoner would have other than his guards. If a prisoner was lucky he would have a chaplain who still remembered what it was to be a priest but some would encounter chaplains convinced in the rightness of the regime and who would spend the last hours of the condemned man's life pointing out where he had gone wrong! One chaplain has written of spending a night with a group of soldiers condemned to death for desertion. Most were glad of his presence amongst them. This chaplain pointed out that he also had a duty to the members of the firing squad as they were just soldiers obeying orders too. Many men called upon to carry out this unpleasant duty found it the most difficult duty of their military lives. The placebo of one man firing a blank round did little to ease the burden and this was where the chaplain was vitally important.

A potent propaganda image: Mass being celebrated for an artillery unit with the field altar placed under the barrel of an artillery gun. The implication of God and might cannot be overlooked as an example of clever propaganda. Courtesy of Chris Liontas.

Chaplains were also expected to help with keeping up the morale of the soldiers. This often took the form of patriotic sermons and we must remember that many chaplains believed in the great crusade against the Godless Bolsheviks. 'God is with us, *and God is with us!* These words are engraved on every German soldiers belt buckle. There is no work that is holier than the defence of our divine Christian values against the scourge of Eastern Bolshevist barbarism. That's what sets the German soldier apart from the Bolsheviks who have no place for God on their belt buckles! You are never alone, even when you find yourself deep inside the enemies territory.'[26] Statements such as this appear ludicrous to us today but to soldiers raised on a diet of Nazi propaganda and racial theory, such a statement from a chaplain made perfect sense.

Many of the senior clergy in Germany also preached strong patriotic sermons about the war in general and especially the conflict in the East. It is part of the role of any priest to preach sermons to boost the spirits of his congregation in difficult times and German clergy took to this task with varying degrees of enthusiasm during the Third Reich. In spite of the state's attitude towards the churches, many Germans still attended services and took comfort in the words of their pastor. However, the pastor had to be mindful that not all of the congregation were there to pray. Many agents of the Gestapo (*Geheime Staats Polizei*) and

Kriegspfarrer Schmidt and some of his congregation pose for a photograph after a service – the chaplain is pictured at extreme left. Courtesy of Chris Liontas.

Dr. Alois Beck celebrates Mass somewhere in Russia. Dr. Beck served later in Stalingrad and survived the war. Another chaplain, who is leaning over the altar, is assisting him in this picture. Dr. Beck wears his priestly robes whilst the assisting chaplain wears uniform and stole. Author

Dr. Beck celebrating Mass at another location, wearing different robes and reading a passage of Scripture to the assembled soldiers. Author.

Dr. Beck consecrates the Holy Communion in the ruins of a church. Author.

A chaplain, dressed in greatcoat and M43 cap, conducts a funeral in the Rorauianni graveyard in March 1943. This was the saddest and all too common task for a chaplain. Courtesy of Oreste Cassoni.

An Army chaplain conducting a funeral for Luftwaffe personnel. Despite the poor quality of the picture, the chaplain can be seen to wear a non-regulation cross. Courtesy of William Dienna.

SD (*Sicherheits Dienst*) also went to religious services to monitor what was being said from the pulpits. Many informers also kept the authorities abreast of any defeatist or anti-party content in the sermons of the clergy. As a result of this infiltration, many clergy feared to be outspoken in public. As a result, much of what has survived the passage of time has been the pro-establishment sermons and pastorals that came forth from time to time. One has to view this with a balanced eye: not all of the clergy were pro Nazi but only the statements of those who were pro Nazi got published and recorded. Those who were openly critical of the regime were dealt with by the *Nacht und Nebel* edict that allowed all those accused of antisocial behaviour or acts against the State to be arrested and imprisoned without trial.

The sentiments amongst senior clergy of the time are recorded amongst the sermons and pastorals of the Bishops during the war. Some were patriotic and prayed for the men at the Front whilst some were openly Nazi and prayed for the scourge of the East to be wiped out in this new 'Holy Crusade.' Some also spoke in condemnatory tones about the Allied bombing offensive against German cities and used the popular term for Allied aircrew – *TerrorFlieger* – terror flyers.

Bishop Rarkowski, the senior Roman Catholic chaplain was very strong in his statements. He believed that the war was just – '*The German Volk knows that it is fighting a just war, one born of necessity of a people's self-preservation*'[27] – and could speak of the Eucha-

In the next series of photos, the role of a chaplain at a funeral is displayed. The chaplain accompanies the officer in command of the funeral cortege. Courtesy of Chris Liontas.

rist and the *Führer* in the same sentence, 'They will distribute the Bread of Life among you, and I am certain that the power of the Lord will come over you and will give you the strength to give your best as soldiers of the German Army for *Führer, Volk and Vaterland.*'[28] The opinion of the good Bishop is quite clear and perhaps understandable as he was from a Prussian military background, a veteran of World War I and a holder of the Iron Cross First class, earned as a chaplain on the Western Front. He welcomed, as did many veterans, the rebirth of the *Wehrmacht* under the guiding hand of Adolf Hitler. The charge has been laid against Bishop Rarkowski that he was the only supporter of the regime and the war. This is unfair as many of the other Bishops also spoke in support of the War. Bishop Clement Von Galen who was very outspoken against certain aspects of the regime was the first Bishop to swear the new oath under the terms of the Concordat signed in 1933. He condemned much of the Nazis activities but was also anti Bolshevik as well! Cardinal Michael Faulhauber viewed Bolshevism as the 'World Enemy' (Nazi terminology) and whilst being outspoken about some of the Nazi practices still allowed warm praise of Hitler in one of his Diocesan papers. Many of the Bishops supported the regime whilst being critical of it. As can be seen from the above brief examples, the Bishops were often quoted as being in favour of the war,

The chaplain reviews the troops as they form up prior to the coffins being placed in the graves. This Army chaplain is conducting the funeral service of fallen Kriegsmarine personnel. It was common practice for chaplains of one service to minister to the other services. Courtesy of Chris Liontas.

The chaplain stands to attention as the coffins are lowered into the graves. Courtesy of Chris Liontas.

The chaplain blesses the graves of the dead, as is common practice in most Christian denominations. Courtesy of Chris Liontas.

The chaplain reads the burial service at the graveside. Unusually, he does not wear a stole/prayer scarf whilst conducting the burial. It is normal practice for one to be worn. Courtesy of Chris Liontas.

Above and following: The chaplain scatters earth on the coffins, reminding the living that, 'we are dust and unto dust we shall return.' Courtesy of Chris Liontas.

especially on the Eastern Front, and anti- Bolshevik. Bishop Rarkowski just happened to be more blunt about it – '*Bless, O God, our Führer and Supreme Commander in all the tasks placed upon him.*'[29]

A very good insight into the role of the chaplain can be found in a German book that lists the experiences of twenty-four Roman Catholic chaplains who served before and during the war. This book is entitled *Mensch, was wollt ihr denen sagen?*[30] – "Men, what do you want to tell them?" The book is a collection of interviews with a cross section of the many chaplains who served as army and navy chaplains both before and during the war. (I cannot recommend this book highly enough to anyone interested in this subject and will refer to the experiences of a number of chaplains interviewed in the book. I will give a general reference to this section as the book is in German and exact page references are beyond the language skills of this author)

Each chaplain paints a vivid picture of his experiences both at home and at the front, as many of them served with combat units engaged in heavy fighting. Whilst each story is different, some common experiences resonate through each of the stories. Above all, the chaplains felt, that as priests, it was their duty to be where the soldiers were, be that at the front, garrison or hospital. A number of the chaplains had the opportunity to leave Germany before and after the outbreak of war but felt that their duty as priests and as Germans was to remain and answer the call of duty, wherever it led them.

Another funeral series of photographs. The remains of the dead soldiers lie in state under an armed guard, draped with the national flag. Author.

A common experience for those chaplains who enlisted early in the war was that there were no formal introductory or training courses for them. Once they passed a medical they were issued with a uniform and posted to their new 'parish' – either a military unit or a field hospital. Later in the war formal introductory courses were in place to prepare the new chaplains for the vastly different world of military life. This was a life that many were ill prepared for. For those who had become chaplains early in the war, in service training courses were provided when time and the military situation permitted. One of the chaplains attended such a course in June 1944 on the Russian Front. Details of the content of these courses are scant but it would have been an opportunity for the chaplains to get together and boost each other's morale. (Some of the clergy rarely saw colleagues, one chaplain claiming to have not seen another priest for two and a half years!) One participant on the course raised interest amongst the other participants because he was a French Monsignor, Comte de Mayol de Lupe who, at 71, was the chaplain of the Legion Voluntare Francaises, more commonly referred to as the LVF. This unit was made up of French volunteers who sided with the Nazi cause against Bolshevism (He has also been linked to the Waffen-SS French Charlemagne Division.).

The flag draped remains, some wrapped in camouflage zeltbahns (tent sections), are carried to the place of burial by a mixture of Infantry and Panzer troops. Author.

The remains are lowered as the officers and chaplain salute the fallen. Author.

A firing party drawn from the Panzer troops fire a volley of shots over the dead soldiers. Author.

Opposite: An elaborate memorial in a church for a son of the parish who had died in action. Presumably he was buried at the front and this was a way for the bereaved family to mark his passing. Above: A funeral for a Gebirgsjager Pionier, the church awash with floral tributes. Author.

Some of the chaplains found being in a uniform a strange experience especially a uniform that did not display rank. The must have indeed being difficult as every military branch places great importance on one's rank and position within the unit. One chaplain was reprimanded by a *Hauptmann* for not saluting him. The chaplain took exception to this as he was of a higher rank to the *Hauptmann* who mistook the lack of shoulder boards for a lack of rank! A nasty situation like this could often get out of hand but thanks to a sympathetic senior officer the matter was resolved.

The chaplains all spoke of how important the attitude of the commanding officer towards their ministry was. If the senior officer was either a committed Christian or was benign towards religious practice, this attitude permeated throughout the officer ranks and the chaplain enjoyed a great deal of freedom of movement. However, if the senior officer was a committed member of the party, the chaplain found himself in a far more difficult working environment. The support of the senior NCOs and especially *der Speiss* (Sergeant Major) also helped as he could make life difficult for those who were abrasive or nasty to the chaplain. Those refusing to attend church parade often found themselves cleaning latrines or chopping wood. A classic example of military evangelism! (Anyone who has served in the military will know that to a lowly soldier, an NCO seems to be more powerful than God, and far more threatening!)

Some of the chaplains had difficulties with the inclusion of the *Führer* prayer in the soldier's prayer book whilst others thought it a perfectly acceptable prayer for the troops.

Grave markers awaiting their graves. Author.

This clearly highlights the different attitudes present within the ranks of the chaplains towards the political situation. Some of the chaplains explained the use of the war flag on altars and communion tables by saying that there was nothing else to use but one chaplain who said 'it was our national flag – why shouldn't we have used it' gave a more realistic and accurate answer. Another chaplain used a Soviet flag as an altar cloth, sewing a cross over the Communist Hammer and Sickle emblem!

The chaplains were very mobile in their ministry out of necessity as many of their 'flock' were stationed all over the place. One chaplain had between 60,000-70,000 personnel under his pastoral care! Usually the chaplains were allocated a car and driver whilst some used a motorcycle. The driver also doubled as the chaplain's orderly and sacristan/verger. A number of the chaplains also rode into the battle zone inside the half-track ambulances that went out to recover the wounded. Above all, the chaplains felt that their place

A garrison chaplain leads a funeral cortege to the graveyard. Author.

The December 1943 funeral of Oberstleutnant Phillip, a Knight's Cross with Oak Leaves and Swords winner of the Luftwaffe. The chaplain leads the prayers at the graveside pictured behind the wreath from the Führer. Courtesy of Chris Liontas.

was in the front and for some this meant the actual foxholes and trenches and others served in the field hospitals. There was no point in expecting to have any credibility with the soldiers if the chaplain only saw them when they were in the rear areas. A chaplain has to have smelt the smoke of war in order to be able to minister effectively to the fighting men, whether he likes it or not!

Any of the chaplains accounts that I have read have emphasized time and again the need for them to be in the front areas and have agreed that their job was made easier by the presence of the 'priest-soldiers' – clergy drafted into the medical units. If it were not for the ministry of these unofficial chaplains, many soldiers would have died without the care of a priest, as it was often impossible for the chaplain to reach the dying in time. As I have said earlier, these 'priest-soldiers' operated with the tacit approval of the senior officers and also with the blessing of the senior chaplains.

A grave marker of a fallen German soldier – standard battlefield style of cross with helmet placed on top but note the symbol on the upright below the name plate. Isn't this a Jewish Star of David? Quite a puzzle! Author.

A post war postcard sold in aid of the German War Graves Association. What is interesting is that the breast eagle on the soldier's tunic and the eagle and swastika decals on the helmets have not been removed from the photograph even though they were now illegal images! Author.

Cooperation between the Protestant and Roman Catholic chaplains was very limited. The chaplains operated quite well as colleagues but didn't take part in each other's services very often. Some of the chaplains shared transport and helped each other out but a number of the Catholic clergy condemned their counterparts for Nazi sermons and being supporters of the regime but this should be read with a careful eye. It is sad to think that the clergy from both churches found it hard to get along when they were serving a regime that had the destruction of both churches firmly in mind. The saying 'United we stand, divided we fall' kept coming into my mind as I read of this un-ecumenical spirit. Some did share in each other's services and ministered to the soldiers who were not of their faith when their own chaplain could not be with them. At the end of the day, when one is facing death and destruction on a battlefield, any blessing is better than none! There is no such thing as an atheist in a foxhole!

Many of the clergy never asked themselves the question 'Is this a just war?'; they felt that their duty was to support the soldiers under their care and that such questions were not relevant to their situation. Yet some of the chaplains felt that there was no such thing as a just war and feared the price that the German people would have to pay after seeing the destruction wrought especially in the East. Those who did not ask if the war was just must have had a strange grasp of justice seeing that a junior seminarian who was drafted during the war felt that capture by the Allies would be a blessing as 'we would be freed from a war which we considered to be criminal.'[31] One chaplain felt that his ministry was just a drop in the ocean but kept going because if he gave up, what hope was there for the men?

4

Chaplain Insignia

German chaplains usually wore military uniform when on duty. This extended to performing many sacramental duties in full military uniform such as funerals, baptisms and weddings. As with all specialists within a military organization, there were a number of items that clearly identified chaplains as such.

Army - *Heer*

To begin this section I will quote from the works of a good friend, *Oberst* Adolf Schlicht. He is the author of the definitive guide to German military uniforms- the *Uniforms and Traditions* series of books:

'By an order (HV 35, No.282) dated 7 May 1935 four groups of chaplains were established:

Heeresoberpfarrer as armed forces officials.

Heerespfarrer with the same status.

Garrison chaplains on full-time jobs (*Standortpfarrer i.H., im Hauptamt*); civilian chaplains on the basis of a personal agreement.

Garrison chaplains with a secondary job (i.e., their main job was as chaplain of their respective civilian parish) *Standortpfarrer i.N., im Nebenamt*; civilian chaplains with a part time job as an army chaplain.

Opposite: A chaplain from World War I on the day he received his Iron Cross Second Class. He wears the chaplains frock coat complete with cloak, chaplains visor cap and large Roman Catholic Cross. There appears to have been little or no regulations pertaining to the style of neck cross worn by Imperial chaplains. Courtesy of Chris Liontas.

Another Imperial chaplain but far different from the previous one! Here is a Franciscan monk serving as a chaplain with the Imperial German Army. He wears his traditional friars robes, vows belt and rosary along with the standard chaplains visor cap and normal Red Cross armband. Courtesy of Franco Mesturini.

The latter two groups were not granted a uniform but rather wore their usual chaplain's dress. By an order (Svol. 7, No.380a) dated 25 May 1937 all civilian chaplains were to be replaced by army chaplains. About 1940 the branch was renamed as *Wehrmachtseelsorgedienst* – Armed Forces Pastoral Service.'[32]

German army chaplains wore the standard officer's uniform of the day – tunic, cap and breeches. This was due to the fact that they were accorded the rank of officer by virtue of their office as chaplain. Buttons for chaplains were in silver, as was normal for officers whereas for bishops all uniform accoutrements, including crosses, were in gold. (Most

An interesting number of photographs all to the same man who served in both World Wars. In this picture Herr Gottfried Bourquin wears the chaplains frock coat, visor cap and chaplains armband. (His armband with Cyrillic lettering appears elsewhere in the book.) Courtesy of Chris Liontas.

Herr and Frau Bourquin pose for the camera. The frock coat can be seen very clearly in this picture. Courtesy of Chris Liontas.

A page taken from his Third Reich Wehrpass that clearly shows his birthplace as Labrador in North America! He is entitled to German citizenship as stated in the Wehrpass but not many people born in America can claim to have served as German chaplains in both wars! Courtesy of Chris Liontas.

bishop's continued to wear their own pectoral cross when in uniform.) Bishop's were also permitted to have violet facings on their greatcoats, in the style adopted by *Generals*. The branch of service colour for German chaplains was violet and can be found on the piping of peaked caps, the *soutache* on overseas caps and on the collar *litzen* of the service tunic. The *litzen* were the same for Catholic and Protestant chaplains except for one difference – the Catholic chaplains *litzen* were mounted on a violet backing as well as having violet in the *litzen*. Protestant chaplains *litzen* were mounted on the same green cloth as other officer's *litzen* and only had the branch of service colour in the horizontal bars again like the regular army officer's. Hence a chaplain's denomination could be instantly recognized even if he was not wearing his neck cross.

The first and most recognizable item of insignia worn by a German chaplain was the cross worn suspended on a silver chain of 76cm around the neck. There were two different types worn; the pattern for Catholic chaplains had a cross that measured 6.1 cm high and 4.7cm wide with the body of Jesus Christ. The pattern for Protestant chaplains had a cross that measured 7.4cm high and 5cm wide and was unadorned except for an outline border.[33] This cross was supposed to be worn at all times whilst on duty but in practice it was often

Another Franciscan chaplain, pictured in 1915 on horseback. This is Feldgeistlicher Walter Emmert of the 1st Bavarian Infantry Brigade He is dressed like the other Franciscan chaplain pictured above but also displays the Iron Cross Second Class ribbon on his monastic habit. Courtesy of Rick Lundstrom.

Three Imperial chaplains pictured in 1917. Two wear the frock coat whilst the chaplain on the left wears a service tunic. Only the chaplain on the right wears the chaplain's armband. All wear the chaplains visor cap. Courtesy of Chris Liontas.

neither possible nor wise to wear it. Wearing a large silver badge around one's neck in a forward area in Russia was just asking to be shot by a sniper.

The chaplain also wore a cross on the service cap, be it the officer's peaked cap, M38 overseas cap or the later M43 *Einheitsfeldmütze*. The cross was worn between the national eagle and the wreath and cockade. Some variations include a separate metal cross, an embroidered wire cross, a BeVo wreath and cross combined and also privately commissioned styles of cross. The official style of cross was a Gothic cross measuring 2x1.7cm of aluminium coloured metal.[34] Again the cross was often not worn in practice but more often than not the chaplain *did* wear the cross on his otherwise standard officer's cap. It has been suggested to me that German chaplains may have worn a cross stenciled on the front of the standard German steel helmet, in the style adopted by some Allied chaplains but this is purely hearsay and included for information only.

Another distinguishing feature of the German chaplain is the special armband worn with the uniform. Under the Geneva and Hague Conventions, chaplains were classed as non-combatants and as such were entitled to wear the Red Cross brassard. However, the

A superb studio portrait of a World War II chaplain with World War I service. He wears the chaplain's tunic with high quality collar patches, a fine example of the chaplains visor cap with Gothic cross. To complete the ensemble he wears the chaplain's armband and Roman Catholic pattern neck cross. The decorations on his ribbon bar are the Iron Cross Second Class 1914, the Prussian War Aid Cross, the 1914-1918 Honour Cross for Combatants and the Army 4 Year Long Service Medal. Courtesy of Chris Liontas.

An opportunity to compare two styles of chaplain dress. Kriegspfarrer Schmidt on the left wears the standard tunic whilst his fellow chaplain wears the officer greatcoat. They are only distinguishable as chaplains by the absence of shoulder boards and the small Gothic crosses on their visor caps. Courtesy of Chris Liontas.

Opposite: A Roman Catholic chaplain salutes as the coffins of fallen soldiers are honoured by a rifle volley. He wears the regulation chaplain's uniform complete with steel helmet and a black stole traditionally worn at Masses for the dead before Vatican II. Courtesy of Robert Noss.

At the front, the spit and polish of peacetime soon vanished. This chaplain wears a greatcoat and cape whilst doing his rounds on horseback – how little things had changed for the chaplain between the wars! He also wears the crusher style of visor cap so favoured by veteran officers. He carries the tools of his trade in pouches on his belt and over his shoulder. Courtesy of Chris Liontas.

German chaplain's armband had an additional band of violet cloth of 7cm that lay on either side of the Red Cross to specifically identify the wearer as a priest. By virtue of wearing the armband, clergy, like medical personnel, were forbidden to wear side arms or carry weapons. However, the field manual H. Dv. 373 dated 18 June 1941 required the wear of pistols by chaplains in enemy countries.[35] This may have reflected the fact that with the commencement of Operation Barbarossa three days later, the chaplains would be entering the territory of a country that was not a signatory to the Geneva Convention, thereby robbing the clergy of their non-combatant status. However, some clergy took the wearing of side arms a little too far, insisting on wearing them whilst taking some services! Chaplains did still wear the armband in Russia and initially spent a lot of time ministering to a people starved of religious freedom since the Bolshevik revolution.

An item of dress peculiar to the chaplain service was the Black Service Dress, which was an over hang from the *Reichswehr* days. 'The black service dress featured a black, single-breasted frock coat (Amtsrock) of a length covering the knees, and with a high collar closed by two hooks and eyes. It was closed down the front with eight (cloth wrapped?) black buttons. The cut of the back was similar to the old style tunics, with a slit up to the waist level, and with two inside pockets. The frock coat was worn with black trousers, black kid gloves, black lace-up shoes, and with either a black top hat or bowler hat. The officer quality national emblem was introduced by an order (HV 35, No.281) dated 25 May 1935, to be placed on the right side of the chest. It was hand embroidered aluminium (gold for bishops) wire on a black backing for chaplains.'[36]

A development of the black service dress was introduced for chaplains to use on formal occasions. This was known as the frock coat. This garment was similar in style to the black frock coat but with a few important differences. The most notable difference was that this frock coat was in field grey materiel. 'The sleeves were with open cuffs, 16cm in height. Eight bright, pebbled, aluminium-coloured buttons were down the front of the single-breasted coat. A 2mm wide violet piping was around the collar, around the upper edges of the open cuffs, along the left front part from the collar down, and often along the right front panel from the waist down. The national emblem was aluminium wire, hand embroidered on a bluish dark-green field. The buttons and national emblems were gold-coloured for the bishops.'[37]

There were two Bishops appointed as *FeldBischofs,* or Field Bishops, during the period covered by this book. I have mentioned the Roman Catholic Bishop before but will give a brief outline of his career. Bishop Josef Rarkowski, a native of Allenstein in East Prussia, was ordained priest in 1908 at the relatively late age of thirty-five and after a curacy was appointed military chaplain in 1914 to the Prisoners of War in Berlin as well as serving as a garrison and hospital chaplain. He also acted as secretary to the Field Bishop at this time until 1916 when he was appointed as a Divisional chaplain to the 1st Guard Divi-

Mgr Beck on home leave in full service dress of a Kriegspfarrer, complete with neck cross, visor cap, and combat decorations. Compare this photo to the one elsewhere in the book of Mgr Beck in his front line uniform. Author via Mgr Alois Beck.

Another studio portrait of a chaplain that gives the reader an insight into the mindset of some of the chaplains of the day. The chaplain is again only identifiable by his cap cross. A cursory glance and one sees a smartly turned out German officer. Courtesy of Chris Liontas.

An Evangelische chaplain poses for the camera with his wife. He also only wears the cross on his visor cap and bears awards from World War I as well as the SA (Sturmabteilung) Sports badge in Bronze. Author.

sion. From 1918 until 1929 he held posts in Koblenz, Königsberg, Breslau and finally Berlin as *Division und Wehrkreispfarrer*. From 1929 he held a succession of posts connected with the military chaplaincy. In 1938 he was ordained as Bishop of Hierocaesarea. (It is a common practice in the Roman Catholic Church for their bishops to hold a bishopric in a region outside of their national boundaries.)

Within two months he was appointed as the Roman Catholic Field Bishop in the *Wehrmacht*. He held this post until February 1945 when he was pensioned off due to the ill health he had suffered since the beginning of 1944. Bishop Rarkowski has been castigated many times in the past as being pro- regime. I would disagree with a lot of the criticism leveled against Bishop Rarkowski and my grounds for doing so are simple. He was a man whose ministry, apart from a short curacy, took place entirely within the military world. He came from a Prussian military background and in light of this, his vocabulary was more suited to the parade ground and staff headquarters rather than the pulpit or theological journal. His pastorals during the war have been heavily criticized but I will repeat what I have said elsewhere. Bishop Rarkowski held views common amongst many of the hierarchy of the day. He was just a little more blunt, or dare I say, honest, in the way he expounded those opinions. Bishop Rarkowski died in Munich in 1950.

An Army – Heer – chaplain conducting a Navy – Kriegsmarine – funeral in 1940. He wears the M38 officer's overseas cap along with standard uniform. Author via Oberst Adolf Schlicht.

Dr. Alois Beck pictured in Southern Russia in September 1942. He wears an Other Rank's M36 tunic – note loops for shoulder boards – and the patches of a Roman Catholic chaplain. He wears the neck cross tucked into the front of his tunic but his peaked cap is minus a cross but is piped in the violet piping of the chaplain's service. Author via Oberst Schlicht.

Opposite: A chaplain poses in a beautifully tailored uniform and cap. He has seen some service as indicated by the ribbon of the Iron Cross Second Class 1939 in his second buttonhole and the loops over his left pocket for a ribbon bar. The cross on the visor cap is an unusual variation in that it appears to be bullion cross embroidered on backing cloth. This is a change from the more common metal cross. Courtesy of Chris Liontas.

The *Evangelisches FeldBischof* was Bishop Franz Dohrmann. He was born in Gross Lubbichow in 1881 and was ordained priest in Berlin in 1908. After his ordination he was appointed as curate to the Holy Ghost Church in Potsdam and in 1909 he became an assistant chaplain to the Guards Division based in that traditionally military town. From 1910 until 1920 he was a Divisional chaplain in Bromberg. From 1920 until 1934 he held the post of *Wehrkreispfarrer* in Stettin. During this period he received various honours from the Evangelical Church and was noted as a leading cleric in the province of Pomerania. From April 1934 until April 1945 he was the Evangelical *FeldBischof* in the *Wehrmacht* and, like his Roman Catholic colleague, also had responsibility for the *Kriegsmarine* as well. Bishop Dohrmann relinquished his post in April 1945 and entered a Benedictine monastery for a short while, possibly to recuperate and later went on to hold a position in a parish in Munich. He retired from the active ministry in 1951 and died in Munich in 1969. Little of his writings or sermons has come to light during this research but given the struggle between the German Christians and the Confessional Church, Bishop Dohrmann must have had a difficult time of it!

A chaplain conducting a funeral in Russia. Note that he is wearing the chaplains armband and a clerical stole. Author via Oberst Schlicht.

In contrast, this chaplain also conducts a funeral but is not wearing the armband. Author.

Above: A chaplain poses with his colleagues from a medical unit. This is an early photograph taken outside a garrison church. Author.

Left: A Roman Catholic chaplain poses in an Italian photographers studio in 1941. He is identifiable only by his neck cross. He has dispensed with the cross on the visor cap. If he removed his neck cross he could be easily mistaken for a German officer. This seemed to be a common practice amongst some clergy in uniform. Courtesy of Franco Mesturini.

The above list of uniforms and accoutrements is not exhaustive and many variations were worn, some official and some unofficial. Chaplains would have been issued or given access to the various summer, winter and other protective uniforms available to the German soldier. As military officials, they would have been under the same regulations but in wartime, not all regulations are followed to the letter of the law. Hence some unusual variations in the hands of collectors and museums. The uniforms described above were the official uniform to be worn but in the field it was often a different matter: 'Padre Peters looked like any one of his comrades. He wore a yellowish sheepskin coat over his greasy tunic, and on his head a grey ski-cap with furry earflaps crowning his stolid countryman's face.[38]

A chaplain on home leave after serving on the Russian Front. He has been awarded the War Merit Cross Second Class with Swords and the Winter War Medal. As was common practice, he has tucked his neck cross into the front of his tunic. He wears a superb example of a chaplain's visor cap. Courtesy of Robert Noss.

Dr. Beck poses with the Battalion staff in 1940. Author via Oberst Schlicht.

Bishop Rarkowski and a number of chaplains pose for a photograph at a clergy gathering. Note that the picture is developed in reverse! It shows the uniformity between the dress of the Bishop and his chaplains. The Bishop and the chaplain to his left display a large number of decorations. Author via Oberst Schlicht.

Navy - *Kriegsmarine*

Navies have been traditionally the most religious of the military services. It has often been said that this religiosity derives from the strong superstitious nature of sailors but is more likely to be due to the fact that the medium in which a sailor works can kill him as easily as enemy action. The *Kriegsmarine* of the Third Reich was no exception. Adolf Hitler recognized this fact when he referred to his navy as a 'Christian navy'.

A Kaiserliche Marine chaplain in civilian dress wears the military armband in a studio portrait taken in 1916. Courtesy of Chris Liontas.

Naval chaplains served both at sea and on dry land. It is doubtful that chaplains went to sea on U-Boats, as the severe space restrictions would have made it difficult for a chaplain's presence to be justified on a working boat. The captain of the U-Boat would have assumed the traditional sea captains role of conducting funerals at sea and the U-Boat base chaplain would make sure that a good supply of religious reading material would be on board to sustain the crew during their war patrol. It is quite possible that the medic – *SanitätsFeldwebel* – was a priest and he then could have looked after the spiritual needs of the crew whilst fulfilling his primary role but this is a presumption on the part of the author.

Originally civilian clergy acted as chaplains to naval bases that were within their parish boundaries. This was to supplement the small number of full time chaplains serving in the *Reichsmarine* – inter-war name for the German navy. Arising out of this practice, there was the unusual sight of uniformed and non-uniformed chaplains working on the same naval

A Reichsmarine (Weimar) chaplain addresses naval personnel at a memorial service. He wears the chaplains black frock coat and service cap. He also wears court-mounted medals earned in World War I, an Iron Cross First Class and a chaplains neck cross. Courtesy of Marineschule Murwik Flensburg

A fine studio portrait of a Kriegsmarine chaplain. Clearly shown are the M1942 collar patches and an interesting variation of the visor cap cross. Courtesy of Marineschule Murwik Flensburg.

Another studio portrait, which shows subtle differences that can be encountered in the same service. A variation of M1942 collar patches and the cap cross is completely outside of the wreath on the visor cap. Courtesy of Robert Noss.

A chaplain addresses the congregation at a graveside – unusually he wears riding breeches and jackboots with his service jacket. Courtesy of Marineschule Murwik Flensburg.

base. By order MV 36, No.126 dated 25 January 1936 four groups of chaplains were distinguished:

Marineoberpfarrer as active officials.

Marinepfarrer with the same status.

Garrison chaplains on full-time (*Standortpfarrer im Hauptamt – i.H*): civilian clergy on the basis of a personal agreement.

Garrison chaplains with a secondary job (*Standortpfarrer im Nebenamt – i.H*): civilian chaplains with a part-time job as navy chaplains with their primary job as chaplains of their respective civilian parish.[39]

By 1937 all of the civilian chaplains were replaced by navy chaplains – Orders vol. 7, No.380a[40]. In practice it is hard for a part-time chaplain to devote much time to his part-time duties whilst also tending to the needs of his parish. The *Kriegsmarine* recognized this fact

An Army – or possibly a Marine Artillerie? – chaplain conducting a Kriegsmarine funeral. Courtesy of Marineschule Murwik Flensburg.

Two photographs showing a Kriegsmarine chaplain conducting a funeral whilst wearing the officer's greatcoat. The greatcoat has the chaplains collar patches applied to the collar and he wears a standard officers belt as well. Courtesy of RM Coverdale MBE.

A chaplain in standard uniform conducts a Marine Artillerie funeral. Courtesy of Marineschule Murwik Flensburg.

A pair of collar patches of the type worn by the senior naval chaplain Marinedekan Ronneberger. Author.

and the role of chaplain became a full-time career, apart from full-time garrison chaplains who remained under specific conditions.[41] A new title was introduced in 1938 of *Marinedekan*, which translates as Marine Deacon and after the outbreak of war; chaplains with the status of wartime officials had the title *Marinekriegspfarrer* – navy war chaplain.[42]

Navy chaplains had worn the standard black service dress as described above for the army chaplains. The clerical collar of the denomination was worn- round collar for Roman Catholic clergy and the pointed collar for Episcopalian clergy that was worn over the stand up collar of the frock coat. The navy chaplains also adopted the national emblem at the same time as the army chaplains. A proper service uniform in keeping with the duties of active chaplains was introduced in 1938 'by order OTB 38, No.9 B.V.A. No.31 III dated 24 March 1938'; a navy blue service dress was introduced for active navy chaplains, but without any distinction between the ranks of *Marinepfarrer*, *Marineoberpfarrer* and *Marinedekan*. By order OTB 38, No.93 III dated 15 April 1938; the chaplains were obliged to wear the uniform.[43]

The furniture on the caps and tunics were all in silver- wreaths, crosses, buttons and so on. As with their army counterparts, rank insignia was not worn either on shoulder boards or sleeves. The uniform of the navy chaplain was that of naval officers with a few additions peculiar to the chaplain. The visor cap was the same as that of officer rank but incorporated a cross at the top of the wreath as can be seen in the photographs in this section. There were as many variations of cross and wreath in the *Kriegsmarine* as there were in the *Heer*! Collectors encounter variations and some can be put down to different manufacturing processes. Suffice to say that the vast majority of navy cap crosses will be encountered as embroidered examples but this should not discourage collectors about metal examples that they may possess in their collections.

The frock coat peculiar to the chaplain service was reissued in navy blue for the *Kriegsmarine* chaplains and seems to have been more popular in this service than with the *Heer* chaplains. A number of the photographs sourced during the research for this book have shown that the *Kriegsmarine* chaplains interpreted uniform regulations with a great degree of personal choice. Many seem to have worn the brocade belt whilst conducting funerals in spite of this being contrary to regulations. The regulation regarding the wearing of side arms by chaplains extended to *Kriegsmarine* chaplains in occupied and enemy territory. *Kriegsmarine* chaplains also wore the same style of neck cross as described above for *Heer* personnel. In conversation with *Oberst* Adolf Schlicht, the question of whether or not the chaplain armband was worn by *Kriegsmarine* chaplains was discussed. During the course of his research for his 3 volume work on the *Kriegsmarine – Uniforms and Traditions of the Kriegsmarine –* information regarding this practice, photographic or otherwise, was not found. This author has also been unable to answer this question in any satisfactory manner.

Front and rear views of visor cap insignia for Kriegsmarine chaplains. The top badge is the regulation type whilst the lower pair are variations. Author via Oberst Schlicht.

A funeral taking place in Denmark in September 1944 – Marine Artillerie personnel act as a guard of honour to fallen comrades. Author.

The Commanding Officer and Kriegsmarine chaplain salute the fallen using the now compulsory Hitler Gruss which replaced the military salute after the July 20 bomb plot. Author.

Above: The officers salute as the coffins are lowered into the graves. Below: The Commanding Officer salutes the fallen. Author.

If *Kriegsmarine* chaplains *did* use the armband, it was out of personal choice and not by conforming to a regulation.

The *Kriegsmarine* chaplain also had his own style of collar patch to identify him. These were far different to the style worn by their *Heer* counterparts. From the introduction of the *Kriegsmarine* uniform until a regulation change in 1942, all chaplains, with the exception of the bishop responsible for the *Kriegsmarine*, wore the same collar patches. This was the case regardless of their status or rank. They were of 'the rhombic form, and made of violet badge cloth – some made of velvet. They were worn as a mirror image pair on the collar. The silver hand-embroidery depicted a laurel leaf wreath of two-thirds the height of the patches, open at the top, and bound together at the base. A Latin cross was centered in the wreath, with its transversal bar in line with the top ends of the wreath. The patches were bordered with a 2mm twist silver cord.'[44]

An order dated 6th March 1942 introduced new rank insignia – with rank distinction – and also career and branch insignia were authorized. The collar patches were 'made of dark blue badge cloth in rhombic form (but 2mm wider than the pre-1942 pattern)[45], and were worn in the same manner as the earlier collar patches on the reefer jacket and also on the greatcoat. 'The wreath was now an oak-leaf wreath (instead of laurel) and the cross was of the Gothic pattern. The embroidery distinguished the ranks as follows:

Marinekriegspfarrer during the first year of service: A silver hand-embroidered wreath partially encircling the cross, and without cord piping.

Marinepfarrer, *Marineoberpfarrer* and *Marinekriegspfarrer* after the first year of service: A silver hand-embroidered wreath enclosing the cross with the leaves nearly touching the top. With a silver 2mm twist cord piping.

Marinedekan: As above, but with gold 2mm twist cord piping.

Dienstalteste Marinedekan: As above, but with gold embroidery and gold twist cord piping'.[46]

In practice, however, the 1938 pattern of collar patches were in use until war's end.

It is interesting to note that the collecting world has seen a large number of collar patches emerge on the market in the past few years for the rank of *Dienstalteste Marinedekan*. A colleague of mine in America has reported that a number of dealers have pairs of these patches for sale at a good number of U.S. fairs. The same patches have also appeared in Europe and I was amazed to see a pair at a fair in Dublin in 2002! As there was only one man entitled to wear these patches and as he would most likely have needed only around 5-

The chaplain scatters earth on the coffins, in keeping with tradition. Author.

The chaplain salutes the dead as the end of his part in the service. A volley of shots would be fired and the traditional song "Ich hat ein kamerad" – "I had a comrade" – would then be sung. Note that the chaplain is wearing his dress brocade belt, contrary to regulations. Author.

A photograph of the same military cemetery on the same day as the above funeral. Author.

A Kriegsmarine graveyard on the Baltic coast. Courtesy of Mark Bentley.

6 pairs for the duration of his service, it would appear strange that so many pairs are now on the market. All of the patches are being sold as genuine and whilst many possibly are, there are, in my own opinion, just too many for them all to be genuine. At the end of the day, it is up to you, the collector, to decide but remember. *Caveat Emptor! Buyer beware!*

Wartime officials in the *Kriegsmarine* wore a badge on their sleeve to identify their role/career. This applied to all trades, including clergy. The insignia for all trades comprised of an eagle, similar in style to the decal on the *Kriegsmarine* helmet and then the specific insignia for the particular trade or career path. The insignia for the chaplain was a row of three pips in a horizontal line. This insignia was worn on each sleeve with the eagle head facing each other when viewed together. Normally this type of insignia would be worn over the rank bands but in the case of chaplains, the insignia was worn on its own. Again the insignia was in silver. The author has no information as to whether or not the *Dienstalteste Marinedekan* wore these insignia but if he did it can be presumed that they were executed in gold. 'Photo studies would indicate that this insignia was rarely worn.'[47]

For the duration of the war, there was only one bishop attached full-time to the *Kriegsmarine*. The two *Heer FeldBischofs* ministered to the Kriegsmarine units in their area whilst retaining their status as Heer chaplains. The *Dienstalteste Marinedekan*, or Leading Navy Deacon in the *Kriegsmarine* was Friedrich August Ronneberger. He had served as a voluntary chaplain at the outbreak of World War I and spent the war serving in a variety of appointments, whilst being promoted steadily up the ranks of chaplain. He ended his war service as senior chaplain to the North Sea Fleet and continued on as a naval chaplain

The remains of British airmen shot down over Germany are being carried into a graveyard by Marine Artillerie soldiers. Courtesy of Mark Bentley.

The officer in charge of the burial detail ensures that full military honours are afforded to the fallen enemy. Courtesy of Mark Bentley.

In the presence of Luftwaffe Flak troops and Marine Artillerie soldiers – possibly the ones who shot the airmen down – RAF aircrew are laid to rest by a Kriegsmarine chaplain. Courtesy of Mark Bentley.

Wreaths in honour of the dead airmen and a Union Jack flag shows the level of chivalry still present in World War II. Courtesy of Mark Bentley.

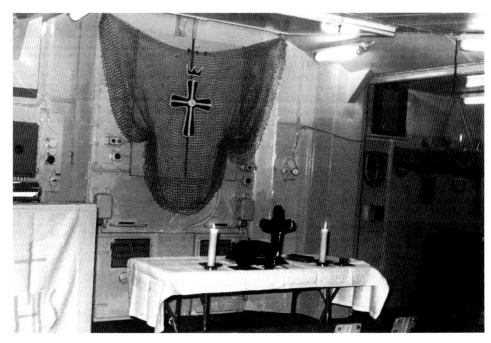

An Evangelisches altar on board a Bundesmarine vessel in the 1970s. Courtesy of Marineschule Murwik Flensburg.

A Bundesmarine chaplain in tan uniform and side cap speaks to sailors on board a German vessel in the 1970s. He is identifiable by the crosses on his shoulder boards. Courtesy of Marineschule Murwik Flensburg.

during the Weimar period. After concluding a stint as ships chaplain on board the Battleship *Deutschland, Herr* Ronneberger became the Station chaplain for the North Sea Marine Headquarters. In 1938 he was appointed *Marinedekan* and on December 11, 1939 was appointed as *Dienstaltester Marinedekan*. He held this post until wars end when he became chaplain to the German Mine Sweeping Administration. He died in 1956. His uniform accoutrements followed the same principle of the *Heer* bishops in that all eagles, buttons, cap cords and so on were in gold and he was also entitled to the violet facings on his greatcoat, in keeping with the practice of all *General*, or in this case, flag (Admiral) rank officers.

5

Chaplain Awards

Unlike their counterparts in the medical service, chaplains were not entitled to all of the awards bestowed upon the military by the powers that be. This was most likely due to the inherent anti-religious attitude of the Nazi establishment. *Reichsführer-SS* Himmler had once gone so far as to try and rob the chaplains of their military status but had to back down when the General Staff intervened. In spite of Chancellor Bismarck's influence, chaplains were highly regarded in the Germany of the Kaiser and many were awarded the Iron Cross First and Second Class during World War I. Many chaplains of the *Wehrmacht* had served as soldiers and as chaplains in World War I and wore the decorations bestowed on them by a grateful Kaiser. Ironically many Jews and clergy who were holders of the Iron Cross perished in the extermination camps, their heroism for Germany conveniently forgotten by the new regime.

During the research for this book I have viewed a great number of photographs of German chaplains and whilst I will never possibly see every photograph ever taken on this subject I have yet to see a photograph of a German chaplain awarded the Iron Cross First Class 1939 – *Eisernes Kreuz Erste Klasse* or *EKI*. I have seen a number of photographs of chaplains who were awarded the Iron Cross Second Class 1939 – *Eisernes Kreuz Zweite Klasse* or *EKII* – and some who were awarded the 1939 bar to the 1914 Iron Cross Second

Opposite: A studio portrait of Kriegspfarrer Schmidt displaying regulation insignia and a privately purchased officer's cap. He displays the following awards: on the ribbon bar the Kriegsverdienst Kreuz Zweite Klasse mit Schwerten – War Merit Cross Second Class with Swords, and the Medaille fur die Winterschlacht im Osten – Winter War Medal. On his left breast pocket he wears the Kriegsverdienst Kreuz Erste Klasse mit Schwerten – War Merit Cross First Class with Swords. It is clear from these awards that this chaplain has seen plenty of active service. Courtesy of Chris Liontas.

A chaplain taking his rest during a lull in the action at the front. He displays the ribbon of the Iron Cross Second Class 1939 in his buttonhole and the Black Wound badge on his breast pocket so it is safe to assume that he has been involved in frontline service. Author.

Class. There seems to have been a wide spread reluctance on the part of the establishment to award the *EKI* 1939 to a chaplain.

I have only found one reference to a chaplain awarded the *EKI* 1939: 'Padre Peter's, the senior chaplain to the division had received the Iron Cross First Class, an unusual distinction for a chaplain.'[48] The rank and file of the army had also noticed how hard it was for a chaplain to earn the Iron Cross First Class 1939.

A more common series of awards to chaplains were the War Merit Cross awards both with and without Swords. An award with Swords was for combat related valour and without Swords was for non front-line valour or meritous service. Chaplains were also awarded the following decorations; Russian Front Medal, Westwall Medal, Occupation medals, Long Service medals, Wound Badges, Sports medals and Campaign shields. Chaplains were also entitled to wear any foreign decorations, which they had been awarded.

One award that has caused controversy since the end of World War II is the so-called 'Chaplains Wound Badge'. Some dealers have sold these badges over the years attributing them to German chaplains from World War I. However, the story behind these badges is far more mundane but still worthy of note. A Roman Catholic monastery – Kloister Weingarten – had been a hospital during World War II and at the end of the war was in a bad state of

A chaplain speaks to a group of soldiers from a swastika draped podium. He wears the regulation neck cross for Roman Catholic clergy but has no cross on his visor cap. He also wears military awards from both World Wars. His ribbon bar consists of the 1914 Iron Cross Second Class, Bavarian Military Service Cross, 1914-1918 Cross of Honour for Combatants. He wears the 1939 Bar to the 1914 Iron Cross in his second buttonhole and also wears the Iron Cross First Class 1914 on his breast pocket. Courtesy of HITM.

repair due to bomb damage and wear and tear. Most *Lazarretts* (German military hospitals awarded wounded soldiers their wound badges during their time recovering from their wounds. As a result of this practice, the Kloister ended up with a lot of surplus Black Wound badges (the lowest grade) at wars end.

The Kloister was a popular place with pilgrims who traveled there to obtain blessings One business minded cleric came up with the idea of using the surplus badges to raise money for much needed repairs. He proposed to remove the centre of the badge thereby removing the swords, helmet and newly illegal Swastika and replace them with a simple cross. The badge was then sold as a religious souvenir of the faithfuls' pilgrimage. This was in keeping with the practice of many Roman Catholic shrines such as Lourdes and Fatima The religious badges proved very popular with the pilgrims and in due course all of the badges were sold in aid of a worthy cause.

This is where the story turns sour. As the post war demand for German badges grew, some individuals began to fake certain badges to fool unwary collectors. One or several (?) dealers of questionable morals and/or knowledge began selling the religious badges as chaplains wound badges from World War I, no doubt equating them with the World War I Army and Navy cut out wound badges that are genuine. Most wound badges are solid on the face

The Roman Catholic and Evangelisches divisional chaplains of a Mountain Troop Division pose for a photograph with the General in command. Both are World War I veterans as evidenced by the chaplain in the centre wearing the 1914 Iron Cross First Class and the chaplain on the right has won the 1939 Bar to the 1914 Iron Cross Second Class. Note that this chaplain is also armed! Courtesy of HITM.

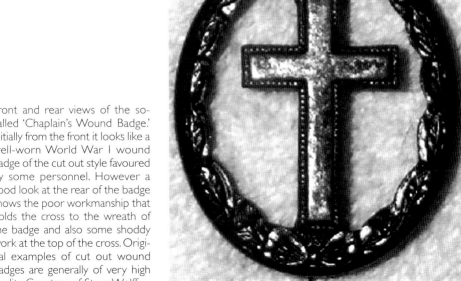

Front and rear views of the so-called 'Chaplain's Wound Badge.' Initially from the front it looks like a well-worn World War I wound badge of the cut out style favoured by some personnel. However a good look at the rear of the badge shows the poor workmanship that holds the cross to the wreath of the badge and also some shoddy work at the top of the cross. Original examples of cut out wound badges are generally of very high quality. Courtesy of Steve Wolff.

but a common practice in World War I was to have a badge with a wreath and a cut out helmet and swords that showed up nicely against the tunic cloth. The cross on the 'Chaplains Wound Badge' was also along this style and hence the story that they are of World War I vintage. Matters have now reached the regrettable stage that this badge is now being faked and as a result people are being sold a fake badge of technically a fake badge!

German chaplains during World War I were awarded the standard wound badge applicable to their branch of service, as evidenced by photographs in this book. If there had been a chaplains wound badge surely examples of the three grades – Black, Silver and Gold – would have come to light over the years, as well as award documents and pay book entries. There would also have been some record of a manufacturer making them or a catalogue such as the catalogue from the firm Steinhauer and Luck selling them. As it is, only black examples of the 'Chaplains Wound Badge' ever come up for sale. This is because the badge is nothing more than a converted World War II black wound badge. In spite of this some dealers will still ask in excess of $150 for an example of this badge.

In spite of the prejudice against awarding the *EKI* to chaplains, you will find photographs of well-decorated chaplains. Many commanding officers recognized the bravery and excellent service rendered by the chaplains and rewarded them as best they could. Collectors can be lucky and turn up an award group to a chaplain but be advised – dealers know the rarity of these groups and will load the cost accordingly.

6

Axis Chaplains

The fact that Germany had a number of allies during World War II is a matter of record and there are many excellent works on the subject. My own look at this area will focus on the related matters pertaining to this work. What *has* been overlooked is the fact that many of the countries that allied themselves to the Nazi cause were fiercely nationalistic and also deeply religious. The Axis of Steel is well known as the tripartite pact between Germany, Italy and Japan. After Germany's initial military defeat of Western Europe, many right wing groups threw their lot in with the German cause. When Germany's war with Russia began in June 1941, more countries allied themselves with Germany in the so-called 'European Crusade against Bolshevism'.

A number of countries in Europe in the inter-war years were passionately Christian and also virulently anti-Bolshevik. The Vatican saw in Soviet Russia the biggest threat to Christendom since the Dark Ages. Many clergy exhorted their congregations to take up the struggle against the ever-growing tide of Bolshevism from the east. This is evidenced by the wave of young men from all over the world who flocked to Spain in the late 1930s to join Generalissimo Franco's forces fighting against the Republican's (who also had their ranks swelled by many foreign volunteers as well.) It has been said that the first shots of the great Nazi-Communist war were fired in the streets and fields of Spain. Many of the Nationalist volunteers entered the hell of battle with the exhortations of their priests still ringing in their ears. Young Irishmen, encouraged by the clergy, fought in a war that had nothing to do with them but confident that they were defending Holy Mother Church from being destroyed by the commissars and workers committees. After a bloody and merciless war, which saw Franco triumphant (heavily backed by Hitler's war machine) world focus shifted as the

Most readers will know that Ita
was part of the Allied side in Wor
War I. This chaplain served with t
16th Infantry Regiment. He is ide
tified as a chaplain by the brea
cross which is red. He is also wea
ing a pistol lanyard! Courtesy
Franco Mesturini.

A peacetime Naval chaplain in the full service dress of soutane bearing shoulder, sleeve and collar insignia and topped off with the traditional Roman hat. Courtesy of Franco Mesturini.

A Bersaglieri chaplain form World War I. He wears his chaplains cross over his breast pocket, contrary to common practice. Courtesy of Franco Mesturini.

An Air Force chaplain form the early 1940s in tropical uniform displaying the standard chaplains cross. Courtesy of Franco Mesturini.

crises of Czechoslovakia, Memelland and Poland dragged the world down the road to world war once more.

In spite of all the help given his side by the Germans during the Civil War, Franco remained neutral at the outbreak of World War II. General Franco went so far as to refuse the demands from the *Führer* for a military alliance. The German invasion of Russia evoked a change in the attitudes of many in Spain. The Nationalists had not forgotten the flow of weapons and material from Moscow that had helped the Republicans fight on far longer than they could have had this aid not been forthcoming. The Nationalists now saw this war as an opportunity to strike back at the Communists on their own soil.

An appeal went out for recruits shortly after the invasion of Russia and by the 2nd of July 1941, when the recruiting offices closed, the numbers who had volunteered were far in excess of the 18,000 required for the Spanish contingent destined to fight in Russia. The recruiting was focused on the Army and the Falange (Spanish Nationalist movement). A large number of the volunteers were drawn from the Falange and the Division took its unofficial name from the colour of the shirts the Falangists wore – a blue shirt. (Much like the Brownshirts of Germany, the Blackshirts of Italy and the Blueshirts of Ireland.) So was born the Spanish Blue Division that fought bravely on the Russian Front, some of its members refusing to return home after political pressure was put on Franco to withdraw the Blue Division. These Spanish volunteers fought with their German allies until the bitter end.

This 1941 group photo shows a monk in traditional habit but also displaying the rank of a senior chaplain in the fascist militia. He has also been decorated many times as evidenced by his large ribbon bar. Courtesy of Franco Mesturini.

An Alpini chaplain poses in a photographer's studio in 1940. Note the chaplains cap badge – a cross enclosed in a wreath. He also wears the standard chaplains breast cross. Courtesy of Franco Mesturini.

An Army chaplain conducts a funeral service for soldiers killed in Albania. He wears a short stole of the style adopted by military chaplains. Unfortunately the front of the helmet is not visible to see if chaplains wore a decal on the front of their helmets, in keeping with Italian practice. Courtesy of Franco Mesturini.

To elaborate any further is beyond the scope of this book. There were a large number of chaplains attached to the Blue Division. It is safe to say that all of the chaplains were Roman Catholic as the population of Spain is predominantly of that faith. Twenty-four members of the Spanish Army's Ecclesiastic Corps volunteered for the Blue Division in 1941.[49] The Spanish chaplains wore standard German Army chaplains uniform with a few national distinctions. In contrast to their German counterparts, the Spanish clergy wore rank insignia on their uniform in the form of a violet patch over the left breast pocket, conforming to Spanish Army regulations. They also wore the sleeve shield of the Spanish Volunteer Division and used the standard Spanish Army chaplains neck cross, that took the form of a wooden cross edged in silver with a silver figure of Christ on the cross (according to Catholic tradition) and suspended by a gold chain. The only other distinctly Spanish embellishment was the Sacred Heart badge that was popular amongst the Army and Falangist volunteers. Spanish military decorations were permitted to be worn and Spanish volunteers were also entitled to German and Axis decorations.

Italy, by some said to have been the birthplace of 20th Century Fascism, had long been an ally of Nazi Germany. Italy is also a deeply religious country, with the Vatican, heart of Roman Catholicism, to be found in Rome. Chaplains featured largely in all branches of the

An Infantry chaplain's portrait, which allows a good look at the chaplains cap badge. His rank is also displayed on the cap. Courtesy of Franco Mesturini.

military and, unlike Germany, in the fascist paramilitary organizations of Mussolini's party. Up until Italy's armistice with the Allies in 1943, Italian chaplains ministered to their own and other Axis troops and many would have carried on ministering to the new allies of Italy. The Italian chaplains by and large wore uniform in keeping with the branch of service to which they were attached. As can be seen in the series of photographs that accompany this chapter, Italian clergy served with many different units of the armed forces and fascist military units. Many clergy remained faithful to Mussolini after the Armistice and served as R.S.I. chaplains until the end of the war.

Peacetime chaplains wore a black soutane with shoulder boards and sleeve rank insignia. On the collar of the soutane was worn the traditional stars of the House of Savoy. Typical clerical headwear was worn, as were military and civil decorations. Some fascist militia chaplains continued to use this peacetime style of dress after the outbreak of war in 1940 (Italy declared war on France just as Germany was about to defeat the French) and replaced the Star of Savoy with the symbol of Italian fascism, the fasces. The fasces were worn on the collar, the shoulder straps and on the crown insignia worn on the hat.

A chaplain to the Naval Regiment San Marco wears traditional soutane and a naval officers beret displaying the naval officers cap badge and rank markings. The stars on his collar are the traditional stars of the House of Savoy. Courtesy of Franco Mesturini.

A chaplain to the MVSN – Milizia Volontaria per la Sicurezze Nazionale or fascist militia – in traditional clerical dress with the addition of shoulder boards displaying the Fasces symbol and rank markings. The fasces is also displayed on his collar and on the cap, which bears a small cross, placed on the rank braids. Courtesy of Franco Mesturini.

A senior Naval chaplain in service 'whites'. The only item to identify his clerical status is a smaller version of the chaplains cross. This chaplain has also been decorated for bravery and service many times. Courtesy of Franco Mesturini.

senior chaplain of the MVSN. He also only wears a breast cross to identify himself as a cleric. He also ears the infamous fascist 'black shirt'. Courtesy of Franco Mesturini.

Another fascist chaplain with the same rank as the previous chaplain. However, he has opted to be pictured in clerical garb. Courtesy of Franco Mesturini.

This chaplain is clearly identifiable. On his tropical Sahariana tunic he wears the standard chaplains badge on his breast but also wears the chaplains insignia on his shoulder boards and cap. An additional feature is the large crucifix hanging from his left breast pocket. Courtesy of Franco Mesturini.

In stark contrast to the previous portrait, this chaplain only wears the breast cross but has also opted to wear a sidearm for his official portrait! Courtesy of Franco Mesturini.

After Italy capitulated in 1943, the RSI or Republico Sociale Italia was founded and many Italians chose to fight on alongside their German allies. This chaplain served with the RSI forces and displays a new style of chaplain's insignia on his breast. Courtesy of Franco Mesturini.

Army, Navy and Air Force chaplains wore standard service uniform along with regular rank insignia. A Red Cross worn on the left breast pocket, and a cross in the centre of the wreath on the peaked cap, *Alpini* hat or traditional *bustina* distinguished army chaplains. Some Army chaplains also wore a distinctive chaplain's badge on their shoulder straps. Navy chaplains used the standard naval cap insignia but did use the red breast cross. Fascist militia and MVSN chaplains wore the standard insignia of their unit but also incorporated the cross into their hat insignia and also wore the breast insignia.

A chaplain of the San Marco Division, wearing the chaplains cap badge, breast cross and metal divisional collar badges. Courtesy of Franco Mesturini.

Two photographs taken of the Spanish 'Blue Division' in Russia in 1941-1942. The chaplain is celebrating Midnight Mass on Christmas Eve for the men of this volunteer division. In the first picture the chaplain blesses the bread and wine at an altar in front of divisional and national flags. In the second picture the chaplain administers Holy Communion assisted by two officers – the divisional sleeve shield is visible on the officer on the left. Courtesy of Chris Liontas.

The chaplain of the Legion Voluntare Francaises – French volunteers in the Wehrmacht – Monsignor Comte Mayol de Lupe. Note the non-standard cross around the Monsignor's neck. Private collection.

(It is interesting to note from the photographs of the Italian chaplains in World War I that there were very little changes made to the chaplains uniform between the wars, apart from the obvious fascist embellishments.)

Many of the eastern European countries that allied themselves with the Nazi cause also provided chaplains to their armed forces. Included in this list are Hungary, Bulgaria, Slovakia, and so on. Details of the uniforms of these chaplains are hard to come by as many were recruited in an ad hoc manner and often devised their own chaplains uniform. Most of the chaplains wore military uniform with some Christian insignia to identify themselves. (Many of the photographs seen during the research for this book show chaplains either garbed in their ecclesiastical robes or wearing greatcoats). A number of the Russian territories over-run by the Germans added soldiers to the anti-Communist struggle. With the newfound religious freedom, chaplains also reappeared amongst the Latvian, Estonian, Lithuanian and Ukrainian troops. Some actually served as chaplains to their countrymen who served in the *Waffen-SS!*

Hungarian troops receiving Holy Communion at a field Mass in Russia in 1942. The chaplain is in his ecclesiastical robes whilst the chaplain assisting him wears standard officers greatcoat. Courtesy of Chris Liontas.

Another aspect of Axis chaplaincy that may surprise some people is the existence of Muslim chaplains to the Axis forces of World War II. Many of the southern regions of Russia invaded by the Axis were predominantly Muslim. Christianity and Islam were equally persecuted by the Communist regime, as was Judaism. The Muslim inhabitants of these regions saw in the invaders an opportunity to shake off the yoke of the hated Communists who punished them for praying to the Prophet. As can be seen in the photographs at the end of this chapter, a number of Azerbaijani soldiers are pledging their allegiance to the *Führer* at a swearing in ceremony. This was carried out by their chaplain, a Muslim cleric known as an *Imam*. The chaplain is wearing a curious mix of uniform; a German officer's uniform complete with foreign volunteer rank insignia, a Muslim turban and a 1908 Pattern British web belt! The troops also display a curious mix of old and new German uniform and insignia.

Another branch of the German forces that had Muslim chaplains was a Division in the *Waffen-SS*- the *13th Gebirgs-Division der Waffen-SS "Handschar"*. This division was raised amongst the many Bosnian Muslims who would not have served alongside their fellow Yugoslavs who were Orthodox Christian or Roman Catholic, the Serbs and Croats. This division was taken onto the strength of the *Waffen-SS* and given its own distinctive uniforms. Their uniforms comprised a typical piece of Muslim headwear, the fez, and the daily

An Estonian Orthodox priest – most likely of the Russian Orthodox Church – celebrates Mass for members of the Estonian SS Division. Estonia briefly enjoyed religious freedom when an ally of Nazi Germany but lost it again after Soviet reoccupation until independence in the 1990s. Courtesy of Chris Liontas.

outine of the recruit was structured to permit time for prayer and the services of an Imam were also made available to the recruits. No photographic evidence of a chaplain in uniform with this division has come to light during the research for this book but that does not mean that no such chaplain existed! A famous picture of the visit by the pro-German Grand Mufti of Jerusalem has been included to show the leeway permitted to volunteers by a German war machine getting more and more desperate for manpower. (Incidentally, the *Freies Arabien Legion* was comprised of a number of the Grand Mufti's Palestinian followers)

One might wonder why Muslim chaplains have been included in a book that deals primarily with Christian chaplains? No self-respecting Muslim would have had anything to do with a Christian chaplain and the foresight of the German hierarchy cannot be over-looked when they were prepared to allow non-Christian chaplains in return for a large in-flux of manpower. Muslims from Azerbaijan, Armenia, Georgia, Turkestan and many other areas enlisted to fight for the Germans. It may also be presumed that the members of the *Legion Freies Indien* would have been afforded the same leeway and allowed the services of Hindu clerics. However this is a presumption on the part of the author and there is no anecdotal evidence to back this up. All that can be said with certainty is that in spite of official state doctrine, the Nazis were willing to turn a blind eye to religious practice in return for loyal fighting men.

The Grand Mufti of Jerusalem, Amin al Husseni, reviews men of the Bosnian Handschar Division of the SS in November 1943. Bundesarchiv.

Azerbeijani Muslim troops swear their oath to Adolf Hitler as they enter the German Army. Most wear the same uniform but display an array of obsolete helmet styles – M16s with and without decals and also an M18 Cavalry helmet. The soldier standing to attention is one of the German cadre of instructors. Courtesy of Gilles Sigro.

A Muslim cleric – Imam – dressed in the uniform of a Leutnant speaks to the assembled volunteers. Most are in uniform but some still appear to be in civilian dress. Courtesy of Gilles Sigro.

A close up of the same chaplain, now in conversation with a German Speiss – Senior NCO. The chaplain wears traditional turban, Leutnants uniform complete with foreign volunteer insignia and what appears to be a 1908 Pattern British web belt! Courtesy of Gilles Sigro.

7

Collecting Chaplain Items

For many years after the war, collecting chaplain items was relatively easy and inexpensive. Many people were unaware of what they were handling and the uniforms, insignia and paperwork of chaplains were not rated all that highly. All this has changed over the past 10-15 years, as dealers are now aware of how rare and collectible chaplain items have become. Some can rightly blame a book like this for increasing the prices of items as information about an item can cause it to become more desirable. This is also often the case after films like *Saving Private Ryan* or *Enemy at the Gates* that get more collectors interested in a particular field. Another problem facing the chaplain collector is that the ever-present fake and reproduction artists have begun to produce chaplain hats, tunics and other items to fool the unwary. Some of the examples of fakes have been very obvious that would fool only a new collector but some are of the highest quality, incorporating many original uniform components to make an item both collectible and expensive. A good friend of mine purchased a visor cap that online looked superb but when held in the hand was nothing more than a reworked Infantry visor cap.

I have seen many fake chaplain caps at fairs over the years and whilst I am lucky to know a good number of fellow collectors and have learned from all of our mistakes, many people collect privately and interact with very few fellow collectors. If a collector like this encounters an unscrupulous dealer, then a lot of money can be spent on items that even a re-enactor would refuse to use for display purposes. (Re-enactors demand very high standards these days. Just look at the prices they pay for reproduction items in the pursuit of historical

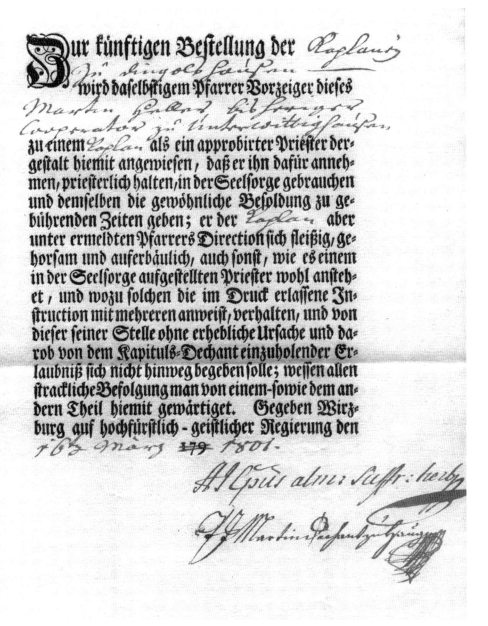

Zur künftigen Bestellung der *Caplaney zu dingolshausen* wird daselbstigem Pfarrer Vorzeiger dieses *Martin Halder helfermyer, Cooperator zu Unterwittighausen,* zu einem *Caplan* als ein approbirter Priester dergestalt hiemit angewiesen, daß er ihn dafür annehmen, priesterlich halten, in der Seelsorge gebrauchen und demselben die gewöhnliche Besoldung zu gebührenden Zeiten geben; er der *Caplan* aber unter ermeldten Pfarrers Direction sich fleißig, gehorsam und auferbäulich, auch sonst, wie es einem in der Seelsorge aufgestellten Priester wohl anstehet, und wozu solchen die im Druck erlassene Instruction mit mehreren anweist, verhalten, und von dieser seiner Stelle ohne erhebliche Ursache und darob von dem Kapituls-Dechant einzuholender Erlaubniß sich nicht hinweg begeben solle; wessen allen strackliche Befolgung man von einem-sowie dem andern Theil hiemit gewärtiget. Gegeben Wirzburg auf hochfürstlich - geistlicher Regierung den *16 März ~~179~~ 1801.*

A letter of appointment for a Prussian military chaplain in 1801. Courtesy of Chris Liontas.

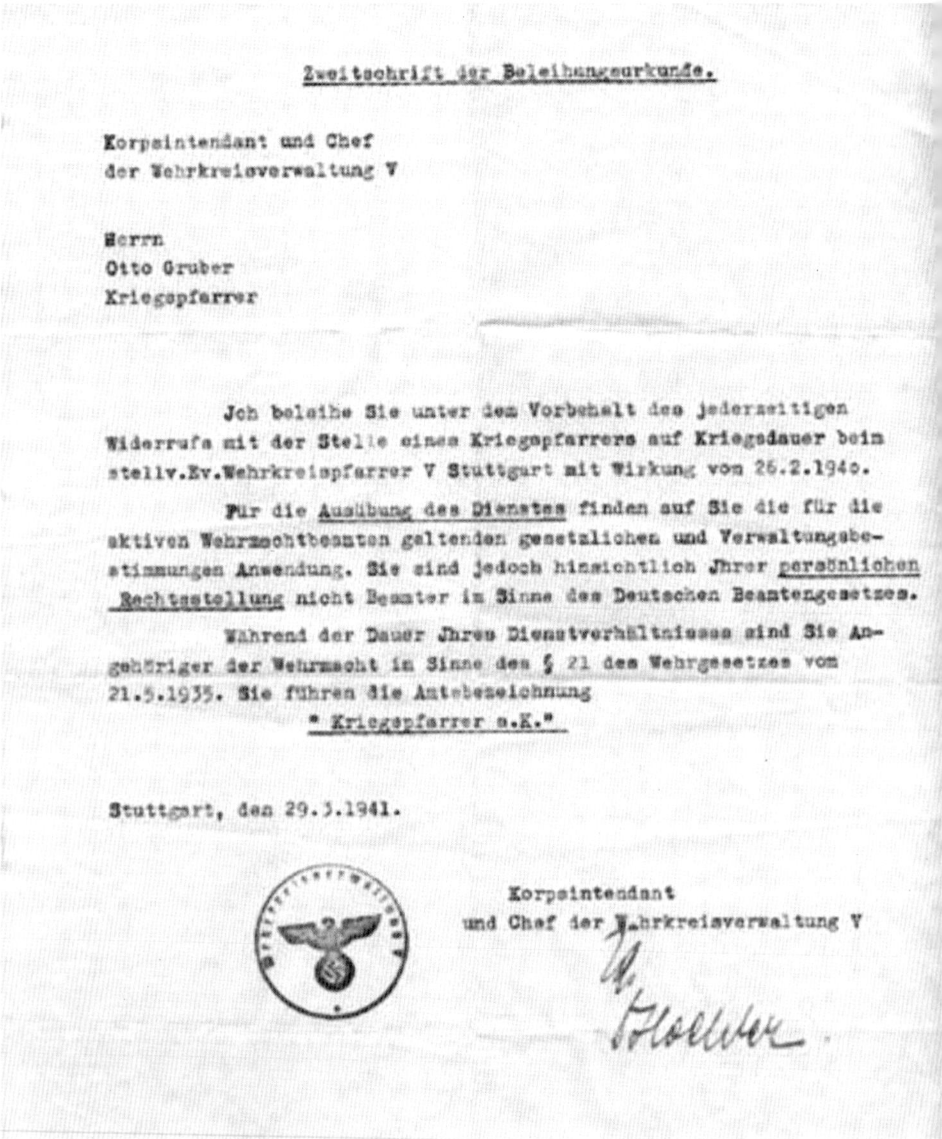

Zweitschrift der Beleihungsurkunde.

Korpsintendant und Chef
der Wehrkreisverwaltung V

Herrn
Otto Gruber
Kriegspfarrer

Ich beleihe Sie unter dem Vorbehalt des jederzeitigen
Widerrufs mit der Stelle eines Kriegspfarrers auf Kriegsdauer beim
stellv.Ev.Wehrkreispfarrer V Stuttgart mit Wirkung von 26.2.1940.

Für die Ausübung des Dienstes finden auf Sie die für die
aktiven Wehrmachtbeamten geltenden gesetzlichen und Verwaltungsbe-
stimmungen Anwendung. Sie sind jedoch hinsichtlich Jhrer persönlichen
Rechtsstellung nicht Beamter im Sinne des Deutschen Beamtengesetzes.

Während der Dauer Jhres Dienstverhältnisses sind Sie An-
gehöriger der Wehrmacht im Sinne des § 21 des Wehrgesetzes vom
21.5.1935. Sie führen die Amtsbezeichnung
    " Kriegspfarrer a.K."

Stuttgart, den 29.5.1941.

                              Korpsintendant
                              und Chef der Wehrkreisverwaltung V

Documents such as the one shown here are very collectable in their own right as they have a strong provenance and are researchable. However, a Soldbuch and a document such as this one, along with awards and/or insignia represent a very good investment and a wonderful piece of history. This is a letter referring to the status of Kriegspfarrer Otto Grusser. Courtesy of Chris Liontas.

ccuracy.) As I have said in my other book – *German Military Ribbon Bars* – items sold as reproductions are perfectly acceptable when they are clearly identified as such but the market is awash with items nowadays that are being passed off as original but are in reality are about as genuine as Adolf Hitler's 1941 London birthday party photos!

A collector wishing to buy a chaplain's visor cap should take a long time to decide on what and where to buy. Buying online is fun and can be very cost effective but when you consider that a chaplain's visor cap in good, untouched condition can vary in price from $1500-$3000, nothing compares to holding the item in one's hands and having a good look at it. Tunics are also very costly, often fetching a price comparable to an SS tunic. Paper work and badges vary in price depending on what the chaplain did and what he earned on the field of honour.

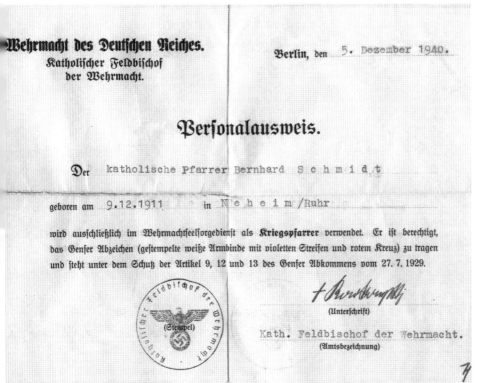

An Ausweis (military pass) for Fr. Schmidt who features many times in this book. This document entitled him to be referred to as Kriegspfarrer, to be in military uniform and also to, 'wear the special armband with Red Cross and violet bands'. It is signed by FeldBischof Rarkowski. Courtesy of Chris Liontas.

Wehrpasses from both World Wars to Kriegspfarrer Gottfried Bourquin, placed on top of his chaplain's armband. Note the Cyrillic lettering, which indicates he served on the eastern Front in World War I. Courtesy Of Chris Liontas.

A close up of the insignia on a chaplains' visor cap. Courtesy of Chris Liontas.

Front and rear views of a veterans stick pin which bears the Gothic cross used by chaplains during World War II. It may be a chaplains' association stickpin but could be something else too! Courtesy of Chris Liontas.

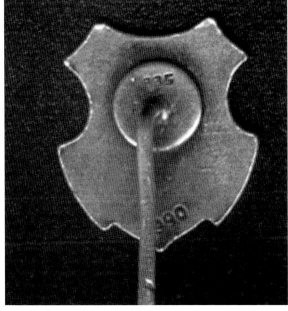

An Evangelisches pattern cross and neck chain in its box of issue. In today's market such a cross can vary dramatically in price ranging from $500 to $3000! Private collection.

'et another variation of Kriegs-
narine cross and wreath for the
'isor cap. Courtesy of Chris
_iontas.

Close up of an Evangelisches chaplains' M38 Overseas cap – minus its national eagle. Many caps were denazified in this way after the war so as not to cause problems with the new authority in Germany. Courtesy of Chris Liontas.

Both caps again, pictured alongside a Pioniers' visor cap. The quality of all three is readily visible. Courtesy of Chris Liontas.

A variety of prayer books, hymn books and Bibles as used by both chaplains and men in active service. Courtesy of Chris Liontas.

The most distinct chaplain item is the chaplains cross and chain. I have seen these crosses offered for sale, complete with box, in excess of $3000. Personally, as a collector who has to save for any big purchase, I feel that this is an excessive and unfair price. Some dealers forget that by pricing collectors out of the market, they are robbing themselves of customers. The chaplain's cross is a simple badge that some dealers have inflated the price of shamelessly. One online dealer recently sold a chaplains cross in good condition, complete with the neck chain for $500, a far more honest price. However, this is just my own opinion. You must decide what you are happy to pay for an item. Having handled a chaplain's cross myself, I saw how easy they would be to fake. There is very little to them and a competent jeweler with an original example to work from would be able to produce a very good copy in a short time and at little expense. I am perturbed at the number of crosses that seem to be appearing for sale worldwide. The crosses have no Nazi insignia so could have been used legitimately after the war and many would have simply been lost over time but,

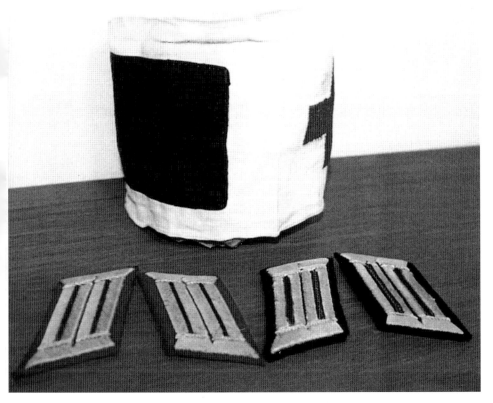

Both styles of Army chaplains collar patches. The Roman Catholic pattern is on the left and the Evangelisches is on the right. The armband in the background is the issue chaplain armband and bore no distinction of denomination. Courtesy of Chris Liontas.

A collage of photographs to show what can still be turned up, if one has the funds and the opportunity! All of these items belonged to Kriegspfarrer Schmidt and represent a valuable collection in their own right both historically and economically. Courtesy of Chris Liontas.

Front and rear views of an Evangelisches chaplain's cross and neck chain. The quality and workmanship is evident in these images. Courtesy of Chris Liontas.

as with the *Marinedekan* collar patches, there seem to be an awful lot of crosses for sale out there today.

One area of chaplain collecting that is still affordable and very enjoyable is collecting chaplain photographs. I began collecting these when *Oberst* Schlicht kindly gave me some copies of photographs he had used in his books. I soon built up a good number of photographs by going to fairs and using a strong magnifying glass to look for crosses and the absence of shoulder boards. You would be surprised at how many photographs of chaplains are still out there and many dealers don't check to see what the subject of a photograph is if it isn't readily identifiable. As recently as last summer (2003) I picked up a set of chaplain photographs at a fair that should have cost me $50-$100 but actually cost me $10. Bargains are still out there for the taking!

Endnotes

[1] The Catholic Church and Nazi Germany, Guenter Lewy, Da Capo Press, USA 2000, Page 85.

[2] Frauen, German Women In The 3rd Reich, Alison Owings, Penguin Books, London, 1995, Page 56

[3] Hansi-The Girl Who Loved The Swastika, Maria Anne Hirschmann, Tyndale Publishing, Illinois, 1974, Page 15.

[4] ' I Was In Prison'- the suppressed letters of German pastors, Charles S McFarland, Fleming H Revell Company, London 1939, Page 12.

[5] Ibid, Page 13.

[6] Ibid, Page 17.

[7] Ibid, Page 18.

[8] Hitler's Third Reich, Issue 28, Bright Star Publishing, London, 2001,Page 12

[9] 7 Op Cit, Frauen, Page 304

[10] Op Cit, I Was In Prison, Page 99.

[11] Ibid, Page 34.

[12] We Were Each Other's Prisoners, Lewis H. Carlson,Basic Books, New York, 1997, Page 51.

[13] Hitler's Pope, John Cornwell,Penguin Books, London 1999, Page 65.

[14] Op. Cit The Catholic Church And Nazi Germany, Page 83.

[15] Ibid, Page 75.

[16] German Catholics And Hitler's Wars, Gordon C Zahn,University of Notre Dame Press, Notre Dame, 1989, Page 72.

[17] Ibid, Page 133.

[18] Ibid, Page 149.

[19] Ibid, Page 14.

[20] Ibid, Page 9.

[21] The Forsaken Army, Heinrich Gerlach,Cassell Military Paperbacks, London, 2002, Page 305-306.

[22] Op. Cit, Hansi, Page 60-61.

[23] Last Days Of The Reich, James Lucas,Arms and Armour Press, London 1986, Page 63.

[24] Voices From The Third Reich, Steinhoff, Pechel & Showalter,Da Capo Press, New York 1994, Page 165.

[25] Ibid, Page 164.

[26] Stalingrad, Johannes Heide,Eurofilm and Media Ltd, 1992.

[27] Op Cit, German Catholics And Hitler's Wars, Page 154.

[28] Ibid, Page 147.

[29] Ibid, Page 160.

[30] Mensch, Was Wollt Ihr Denen Sagen? Pattloch Verlag, Augsburg, 1991.

[31] Op. Cit. We Were Each Other's Prisoners, Page 148.

[32] Uniforms And Traditions Of The German Army, Vol.2, Adolf Schlicht &JR Angolia, R James Bender Publishing, California, 1986, Page 168.

[33] Ibid, Pages 169 & 172.

[34] Ibid, Page 174.

[35] Ibid, Page 166.

[36] Ibid, Page 168.

[37] Ibid, Page 173.

[38] Op. Cit The Forsaken Army, Page 102.

[39] Uniforms And Traditions Of The Kriegsmarine Vol 2, JR Angolia and Adolf Schlicht,R James Bender Publishing, California, 1991, Page 231.

[40] Ibid Page 231.

[41] Ibid, Page 231.

[42] Ibid, Page 231.

[43] Ibid, Page 233.

[44] Ibid, Page 237-238.

[45] Ibid, Page 238

[46] Ibid, Page 239-240.

[47] Ibid, Page 240.

[48] Op. Cit, The Forsaken Army, Page 26.

[49] Germany's Spanish Volunteer's 1941-45, John Scurr,Men at Arms Series 103, Osprey, London, 1980, Page 39.

Bibliography

Primary Sources

The Catholic Church and Nazi Germany, Guenter Lewy, Da Capo Press, New York, 2000

Frauen, German Women in the Third Reich, Alison Owings, Penguin Books, London 1995.

Hansi – The Girl who loved the Swastika, Maria Anne Hirschmann, Tyndale Publishing, Illinois, 1974.

I Was In Prison – the suppressed letters of German pastors, Charles S. McFarland, Fleming H. Revell Company, London, 1939.

We Were Each Other's Prisoners, Lewis H. Carlson, Basic Books, New York, 1997.

Hitler's Pope, John Cornwell, Penguin Books, London 1999.

German Catholics and Hitler's Wars, Gordon C. Zahn, University of Notre Dame Press, Notre Dame, 1989.

The Forsaken Army, Heinrich Gerlach, Cassell Military Paperbacks, London 2002.

Last Days of the Reich, James Lucas, Arms and Armour Press, London, 1986.

Voices from the Third Reich, Steinhoff, Pechel and Showalter, Da Capo Press, New York, 1994.

Mensch, Was Wollt Ihr Denen Sagen?, Pattloch Verlag, Augsburg, 1991.

Uniforms and Traditions of the German Army Volume 2, Adolf Schlicht and J.R. Angolia, R. James Bender Publishing, California, 1986.

Uniforms and Traditions of the Kriegsmarine, J.R. Angolia and Adolf Schlicht, R. James Bender Publishing, California, 1991.

Germany's Spanish Volunteers 1941-45, John Scurr, Men at Arms Series 103, Osprey, London, 1980.

Ireland during the Second World War, Ian S. Wood, Caxton Publishing, London, 2002.
Feldgrau, Franco Mesturini and Luca Soldati, Ermano Albertelli Editore, Parma, Italy, 1995
Eyewitness War – personal accounts of World War II, Marshall Cavendish, London, 1995.
German Wound Badges 1914, 1936, 1939, 1944, 1957, William E. Hamelman, Matheus
Publishing, USA.

Secondary Sources
Hitler's Third Reich, Bright Star Publishing, London.
Military Illustrated, Publishing News Ltd, London.
The Armourer, Beaumont Publishing, Cheshire.
Stalingrad, Johannes Heide, Eurofilm and Media Ltd, 1992.

Index